AGE OF
CONVERSATION 3

IT'S TIME TO GET BUSY!

EDITED BY

Drew McLellan and Gavin Heaton

Channel V Books
New York

Interior design: Gavin Heaton
Cover design: Chris Wilson

Published in the United States by Channel V Books,
a division of Channel V Media, New York, NY.
www.ChannelVBooks.com

Channel V Books and its logo are trademarks of Channel V Media.
ISBN 978-0-9824739-4-8

Library of Congress Control Number: 2010904822

Library of Congress subject headings:

Marketing.
Social media.
Internet marketing.

PRINTED IN THE UNITED STATES OF AMERICA

10 9 8 7 6 5 4 3 2 1

First Edition

Note from the Editors

This book almost didn't happen.

We discussed creating a third edition of *Age of Conversation* but neither of us showed a great passion for it. Perhaps the two earlier books had served their purpose. Perhaps they were "of their time" and there was simply nothing further to be said.

But as 2009 stretched onward, it felt like there was something missing. Authors from the previous editions were publishing their own books. Blogs continued from strength to strength. And social media began to gain a serious foothold within the businesses of corporations across the globe.

And yet.

And yet, the individuals within the community fostered by the previous two books continued to thrive. Sure, it was great to see the brilliant thinking of our colleagues making waves. But for every new blog post we read and every new book that was published, it felt as though there was an ever-greater distance between all of us. It felt as though we needed to produce another *Age of Conversation* to again showcase the intellectual and creative power that comes from this crowd.

This edition is, again, different from the previous two. We have been more proscriptive in the curation of the content and more exacting in its ordering. We have edited judiciously. And we believe that this is the most comprehensive work thus far.

As with the previous books, we have received contributions from all over the world, and we thank each author for not just their creative and intellectual efforts, but also for their generosity. The sections covered in this book are:

- At the Coalface
- Identities, Friends and Trusted Strangers
- Conversational Branding
- Measurement
- Corporate Conversations
- In the Boardroom
- Innovation and Execuiton
- Influence
- Getting to Work
- Pitching Social Media

— Gavin and Drew

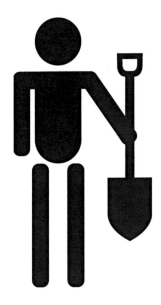

At the Coalface

Crowdsourcing for a Country We Love

Sacha Tueni and Katherine Maher

"Sure, I've heard about citizen reporting. All the media companies keep trying it. It doesn't work."

Those were the "encouraging" words of the old guard — an executive at a venerable Middle Eastern media and publishing house.

Lebanon was weeks from pivotal parliamentary elections and everyone was preparing — the political parties, the media — and a group of volunteers was working to launch Sharek961.org.

Sharek961 (*Sharek* translates as 'Participate!', +961 is Lebanon's international dialing code) was built as a citizen — and civic — reporting platform. In Lebanon, a country characterized by partisan political and media fiefdoms, neutral news is elusive. Sharek961 encouraged Lebanese citizens to participate in civic society by sending first hand reports on election issues. Reports would be tagged — with location, source, and category — and published on Sharek961.org as well as over Twitter and RSS.

Launching Sharek961.org with open source tools Ushahidi and FrontlineSMS was simple, and web and grassroots partners spread the word. The platform handled multiple channels: SMS, email, web, and Twitter. The logistics were solid, the volunteers were eager, and the election was days away.

That's when things became difficult. *Could we convince people of their anonymity* (and safety)? What if reports were false — intentionally misleading "poison data" or just bad information? What was our responsibility to act on or share information with authorities? And of course — what if Sharek961 is used for incitement? Anonymity was a major concern — could people report malfeasance without fear of retribution? Yet anonymity removed accountability and invited abuse. Although anecdotal evidence suggested users were tech-savvy — first contributors and first distributors — who already used anonymizing techniques, we scrubbed identifying information. Validity was another challenge — although eager to see reports redistributed, we knew that repetition lends latent credibility even to false reports, and we prominently tagged inflammatory news as unverified. Moderating these reports wasn't an option — it implied editorial oversight and undermined neutrality. Our solution was context and volume — related reports and corrections were appended to the originals.

User feedback and media coverage was enthusiastic but we never lost sight of the hazards. Our approach was to think about implications for risk — real risk — at each stage. It wouldn't stop us doing it again — we believe it's more important than ever. Unambiguous objectives and standards were our guides, and allowed us to bring citizen reporting to Lebanon.

SHAREK961.org

Old Proverb: Listen Twice as Much as You Speak

Gary Cohen

More than ever, we have to stay in tune with our audiences. And that has never been easier or harder than it is now with social media. Tools abound but the key elements we have to work with are attitudes and time. Within small to midsize companies who are enamored of social media and an expectation of low cost and high reward, the results are often seen as disproportionately low on in-house social media efforts when compared to the time and dollars expensed.

A piece by The Union of Concerned Scientists on coal concludes:

> Despite all of these advanced techniques, it may never be possible to produce energy from coal without carbon emissions. Most of the heat produced from coal is generated from carbon, which provides more than 70 percent of the energy content. Since there is so much coal in the world, and the cost of extracting it is so low, it will take a concerted effort to avoid massive carbon emissions. More efficient use is a start, but replacing coal with renewables is the ultimate solution to the environmental impacts of coal.
> — http://www.ucsusa.org/clean_energy/coalvswind/brief_coal.html

Rewording the paragraph to relate to social media at the coalface would look something like this:

> Despite all the advanced techniques and technologies, it may never be possible to produce consistent social media ROI without building flexible strategies and integrating traditional components. Results produced from social media efforts are generated from people and content through community platforms familiar to audiences. Since there is an abundance of social media platforms and conversations which small and mid-size business owners incorrectly perceive as a low cost option, it will take a concerted effort to avoid consistent disappointment when identifying, connecting to, or seeding a conversation through social media compared to the reach of traditional approaches. More efficient use is a start, understanding that at the coalface of social media things are evolving so fast that the ultimate solution to the social media impact lies not just in the execution, but in the ability to flexibly adjust and execute in relation to market and audience changes.

A social media policy is not just a way to protect an organization – it is also a way to educate its members. For small and mid-sized businesses, it helps bridge a "social media" generation gap to bring a company into the 21st century.

GARYDCOHEN.com

Quote from The Union of Concerned Scientists briefing, *How Coal Works,* is reproduced with permission.

The New Interpreters

Amber Naslund

In the real world, change isn't instant. Ever.

But social media has whipped many folks into a frenzy about the possibilities, losing sight of the here and now, and the path between the two.

There's no question that the Age of Conversation has harnessed a new mindset, new intentions for business (or, as some might argue, a return to some more fundamental principles of customer focus and communication). But in our sometimes unbridled enthusiasm, we've set loose a herd of hyper-connected bulls in the China shops of our existing businesses.

As social media advocates, we need to take a calm, focused, and realistic approach to wiring social media into our organizations. It's our job now to steward our knowledge, share it internally, educate others on what we believe to be true and why it matters. We are the interpreters of a new language, the ambassadors for a shift in operations, in culture, in communication. And it's not going to be easy work.

We need to remember that there's more than one set of vocabulary in any given business, and not all of them translate easily. Our new language is fraught with fuzzy terms like "transparency" and "authenticity" and "being human" on the web, but few of those phrases mean a lick of anything in a business. Sit in the management meeting or the C-suite and throw those words around, and watch your buy-in disappear faster than you can blink.

In order to gain credibility for this new media evolution we want so badly, we have got to start putting it in in terms that our colleagues, teams, and management can understand. It's up to us to provide concrete illustrations for the visions we have, and sound explanations for how our take on social media strategy and application will translate into forward progress toward larger goals.

That means realizing the impact points that social media might have, outside the vacuum of our discipline or department, both operationally and culturally. Building coalitions of our peers to discuss, strategize, plan, and set measurable goals. Sitting down at the table with the skeptics, the contrarians, and the risk averse and openly addressing their concerns. And doing all of this with a calm, dedicated, and long-term focus on the end, not the means.

We are passionate pioneers, and we believe something transformational is happening around us. But let us be stewards and diplomats, business people and pragmatists. Let us be the interpreters of this new language, and put confident voices of reason behind our resolve.

ALTITUDEBRANDING.com

The Fate of Grapes and Raisins: What to Expect When You Add Social Media to the Communications Mix

Iqbal Mohammed

What happens when you put a raisin in a bowl of water? It takes in water and swells up. And what if you put a grape in sugar solution? It loses water and shrivels up.

Try and replicate the same experiment with a coconut and, predictably, nothing happens. The coconut remains unchanged.

What's happening in the former (and not in the latter) is osmosis — defined as the net movement of water across a "semi-permeable" membrane. Osmosis is the primary mechanism by which water is transported in and out of cells and it continues working until solvent concentration is equalized on either side of the membrane. Crucially, it requires no external energy input to function.

In this context, a coconut is a good model of a modern company. It has an information-rich core with a hard impermeable boundary — designed to keep inside information from going out and outside information from flowing in freely. This hard shell consists of confidentiality clauses, NDAs, patents, trademarks, organizational hierarchy, role definitions and boundaries, legalese, PRspeak, etc.

When information does flow in or out, it is only after being cleared and vetted by designated gatekeepers — commissioned research from the outside in; advertising and PR releases the other way around.

But what this artificial regulation of the otherwise free-flow flow of information — information osmosis, as it were — does is introduce energy into the equation. This regulation often comes at an enormous cost — of energy, effort and expense.

Embracing social media is in effect the voluntary act of trading this expensive hard casing for a permeable layer of skin. If implemented correctly, a social media undertaking enables two-way information osmosis — and in the spirit of osmosis, requires little or no energy to keep going. (If not implemented insincerely, as happens often, a social media tactic becomes just another expensive communication effort, an old-style information control device in the guise of a shiny new object.)

Seen this way, a social media exercise is a choice a company makes to remain in "sympathy" with its surroundings — continually effecting organic change on its environment and likewise remaining intimate with its ecosystem to be affected, without any delay, by any changes in the marketplace.

The hard part here is not organizing or enabling the flow of information — in either direction. The hard part is the change of skin — and that usually has to begin with a change of heart.

MISENTROPY.com

6

Lessons Learned from an Unsuccessful Social Media Campaign

Julian Cole

Problem

Yves Klein Blue (YKB) are an indie/rock band who in June 2009 were about to release a new album, *Ragged and Ecstatic*. With the release of the new album it was hoped that it would become a Top 40 selling album.

Strategy

To capitalize on the growing success YKB were having with Twitter, we decided to leverage a Twitter application which allowed someone to download an mp3 when they tweeted a unique code — this had been used by TRV$DJAM weeks earlier: see trvsdjam.com.

We proposed that YKB would allow people to download one of their songs and go in the running for VIP tickets to the Splendour in the Grass event if they tweeted a specific code: see splendourinthegrass.com.

Implementation

We used Culture Jam who built the original TRV$DJAM application to build the site and application for us: see culturejam.com. For launch, we reached out to YKB's existing social network and communicated the offer. We then contacted a number of influential music tweeters/bloggers and made them aware of the offer.

Results

We were hoping for 1200 downloads of the song. This was based on an estimation that 15% of their current social network followers would tweet the offer and that they would influence one other person to do the same. We ended up falling significantly short of this target with only 432 downloads of the track.

The silver lining was that we were able to double the size of YKB's Twitter following — they went from 487 to 1017 followers in three weeks. It took five months to get their first 487 followers.

Learnings

Size of Twitter in Australia
Twitter is really, really small in Australia. Twitter has 250,000 active Australian users. That is nothing! That is 3.5 percent of the size of Facebook. When you are trying to find a niche audience of fans, it probably would have been better to not make it even harder for ourselves by launching on a niche social platform such as Twitter.

Mix of Earned and Paid Media
We can't rely on word of mouth to drive traffic to an application. We realized that successful social media campaigns require a mix of earned and paid media for an idea to kick off in the social media environment.

Comparing the Australian and US Audiences
Be cautious when making comparisons between the US and Australia. Travis Barker and DJ-AM at the time had a substantial following, YKB did not.

What Works for Me

Simon Payn
||||||||||||||||||||||||||||||

It's the Social, Not the Media
I avoid concentrating on any particular medium, be it blogging, Facebook, Twitter, email … or the phone.

For me, it's the social that counts, which means three things:

1. Providing valuable content
2. Listening to what people say
3. Replying and providing solutions

Value is King
I've found that the more valuable content I provide, the more conversations I start. So I think before every post: is this really adding something to the conversation? Is it worth my readers' time? Is this content honest, truthful and personal?

Ask, If You Want to Get
If I really want to start a conversation, I've found I have to ask questions. Some people will respond anyway, but many more will respond if you directly ask them to.

So, if I want to start a dialog on a particular topic, I pose direct questions, such as, What do you think about this? Do you agree with me?

Don't Forget the Phone
Despite the internet, the phone is still one of the most effective ways of starting a conversation. It's faster, more efficient — and more personal. When I put a phone number on my website, my business increased. Some people just like communicating that way.

Act on Some Suggestions
I survey my customers every six months. I get lots of product ideas (and testimonials) by doing this. It's important, however, to act on suggestions. People notice it when I do (and thank me). It makes them more likely to make suggestions next time.

Don't Act on Some Suggestions
Just because someone suggests something, it doesn't mean I have to act on it. While it's nice to be responsive, I also remember my overall business strategy. If acting on the suggestion isn't going to drive my business forward, it's best to leave it alone — even if that means I cannot satisfy one customer.

Some People Talk — Some Just Listen
Some people enjoy conversations — they become real followers of what I do. But not all those followers turn into buyers. Others never have a conversation — but they keep buying from me.

So while conversations are a good thing … words don't always turn into cash. And, of course, you need paying customers to sustain a business.

||||||||||||||||||||||||||||||||||||||
SIMONPAYN.com

8

Measuring Social Media?
Do It with Context

Jye Smith

When it comes to social media, it's all about measuring "engagement" and everyone wants a definition of what "successful engagement" is. I think a better way of looking at it is measuring the business outcomes that are fuelled by social media activity.

These are the steps we take to determine how to measure engagement, influence or whatever you want to call it — it comes back to measuring whether we're reaching a business outcome.

1. Look at success, understand what it is
2. Understand why you want to get there
3. Ensure it meets the business outcome
4. THEN decide how you're going to measure it.

Four steps — no more, no less.

Know Your Objective, Know Success

In the ultimate quest of *Lord of the Rings*, everyone in the Middle Earth knew they were after the Ring. The Fellowship had a clear objective: destroy the ring and save the world. Meanwhile, those seeking power had another goal in mind: use the ring against those who are beneath you. (And the underlying message is, whether good or evil, if we work together, we'll get there.)

Both sides had a clear desired outcome, the objective.

Above all, in your social media engagement, you need to always have clear outcomes and objectives in mind. Whether you work in community management, PR, marketing or administration: your purpose exists.

Define success. Make sure you understand what you value. And if you're doing good work, let others know about it. If you can't articulate what you're doing — then how can you value it?

Measure "Useful Stuff" with the Right Tools

I learned so much from joining the Switched On Media team because their search guys knew so much about reporting for SEM and SEO. Currently, we use up to 12 different tools for social media reporting depending on what the client values and wants to measure. Measuring tools are changing all the time and I don't know what the tools are going to look like in 6 months — but I still know what I need to measure.

Measure with Context

Identify what you are measuring, and why you are measuring it: and make sure that social media activity leads to a business outcome. Focus on this relationship between social media activity and business outcomes – and your measurements will help you move towards your goals.

Becoming an Eventual Expert

Stanley Johnson

Spend any time on Twitter and you'll soon see that there is no shortage of people proclaiming themselves to be experts in social media. Like any emerging area of interest, if there is money to be made you're sure to find more than a few gold diggers.

Yet, as far as I am aware, social media is not an area of specialty you can study at college or university. So if these so-called experts have no recognizable qualifications, why would any marketer trust them?

Especially when you know that all it takes to become an expert in social media, at least as far as I can see, is a blog or Twitter account. Plus a fair amount of ego.

So if you can't trust the "experts" who can you trust?

Well, therein lies the conundrum that is social media. You can't trust anyone. Yet you have no choice but to trust everyone.

Why?

Because practitioners of social media, much like their clients in marketing departments, are learning each and every time they undertake a campaign.

Which means there is always an element of risk involved.

And in order to do something different, new or out of the ordinary, you need to be prepared to take that risk. Sadly many marketers are not.

They like to stick to the tried and tested. The stuff that has worked before. Ideas that will result in a pat on the back not a kick up the arse.

It takes a brave client to give social media a real go. And brave clients are hard to find.

Sadly, the petty bickering and backstabbing that pervades social media circles isn't helping.

Being brave enough to undertake a social media campaign is one thing. Being tough enough to withstand the shit-storm that follows if the so-called experts don't like it, is something else again.

And as a person at the coalface, let me tell you that that is not an exaggeration, it is a statement of fact.

I held the hand of a client as they dipped their toe into social media. What followed was not pretty. But we helped them weather the storm.

They learned. We learned. And we will use our collected learnings for their next campaign. Until, eventually, we have learned enough to call ourselves experts.

BRANDDNA.BLOGSPOT.com

Building a Business, One Question at a Time

Karin Hermans

Working at the coalface on Social Media. To me that means doing what we have been doing for some years now: using the principle of social media — interaction between readers and writers/consumers and businesses — as an integrated part of not just our marketing but of our way of being in business, building our business.

Foundation

We love questions. Better still, we love to answer questions.

Our Social Media "adventure" started by joining in two DIY forums and answering questions related to natural wooden flooring: how to install, how to select the best floor, how to prepare for the installation, how to maintain the floor etc. Our business name is our nickname and our profile links to our website, so no hidden objectives.

First Floor — No Pun Intended

Answering questions is addictive, so on our blog (see faq.woodyoulike.co.uk) — launched in September 2006 — we opened up the comment box for questions. And they came, in droves. There were so many questions, we could fill most of our further posts with articles that went deeper into the answers we gave in the comment box. And those new posts triggered more questions from those with slightly different problems or in slightly different situations. So we answered them too and wrote more posts.

Stairways

Then, using AWeber autoresponder, an email marketing tool, we offered on/offline personal advice — submit your question online and receive a personal answer in your inbox. Again, this gave us much more material to write about.

While our blog, static website, knowledge base and incoming requests for advice grew with these Q&As, we started bundling frequently asked questions into guides.

Extension

We are now in the process of building our own "membership-site" — for lack of better word — where those who buy one of our guides can not only read the lessons/articles on how to select, install and maintain or repair a floor, they can again ask questions underneath every lesson/article which we will answer (and use to improve our articles), they can even interact with other DIY-ers, sharing their experiences and knowledge.

Questions have built our expertise; answers have built the perception of being the expert. One question and one answer at the time.

Roof?

There's no roof as far as we are concerned, the sky is the limit. We just continue to build our business: one question and one answer at the time.

THEKISSBUSINESS.co.uk

How Do I Get My Boss to Buy Into Social Media?

Mark W. Schaefer

In my position as a teacher and consultant, this is one of the most common questions I hear. Here are four ideas to get the boss on-board.

Conduct a "Pilot" Program

Go to your boss and tell her you want to try a new idea for 12 weeks (which sounds shorter than 3 months!). Explain that you will do this as an added, incremental effort that will not interfere with your normal job duties, you will measure and re-evaluate at the end of the period, and together you'll decide whether to continue or not. Once the effort gets going and gains momentum, it's going to be difficult to stop unless you completely blow it. So don't blow it. :)

Money Really Does Talk

Whatever you do, don't go into a meeting with a company executive explaining that you want sponsorship to measure your company's "quality of conversations." If you are still buying into the "it's all about the conversation" hype, read more about ROI and measurement — everything measured in an organization *somehow* relates back to money, whether it's profits, donors or funding. Social media is no different. Be prepared to explain how your initiative ties to the company's objectives. If you can't, you're not ready for this discussion.

The Small Victory Strategy

Plan your social media pilot program around easy "small victories" (SVs). An example: "By week one, we want to have 100 followers, by week 2 we want to have 25 mentions, etc." Notice how different this is compared to "we want to increase our customer satisfaction rate 28 percent by 2012." Small victories allow you to announce lots of happy news when you need it most — at the *beginning*! People will get behind a winner. Establish a culture of support and enthusiasm by building easy wins into the program and promoting those SVs every week!

Plan for Problems

When implementing change in an organization, it's important to have a counter measure for every obstacle you're likely to face. Literally write down every possible argument and reason people will argue against your social media proposal and then formulate a reasonable counter measure to address them. Get your supporters to help you think through effective answers to anything your boss can throw at you and be well-prepared.

BUSINESSESGROW.com

Listening at the Coalface

Katie Harris

There's a lot of hype around social media monitors (SMMs). Not surprising really. Getting feedback on the cyber-buzz around your brand, product or service, from the coalface itself — great idea! But there are two things to keep in mind when using SMMs for market research; sample and sentiment.

Sample

A SMM research "sample" comprises the searchable/findable content found via online channels. That's as precise as you can get. Because beyond the obvious (or not so obvious) skews, there's just no way of knowing who is (or isn't) represented within that content.

For example, SMMs can't automatically distinguish between content generated by core vs. infrequent vs. non-customers. Or marketers for that matter. In effect, all customer/brand relationship variations are given the same share of voice and weight.

Sentiment

Sentiment is often *the very essence* of what we're trying to understand through market research. But this is something that SMMs don't gauge very well for two reasons; accuracy and specificity.

Accuracy

As an example, take the words "F&*#ing brilliant." Depending on the *context*, these words could be:

- Dripping with irony
- An exclamation of genuine excitement/joy
- A description of a high-wattage light bulb

So, would it be labeled as negative, positive or neutral? See the problem?

Specificity

But even if we could achieve 100 percent accuracy in labeling sentiment, broadly defined labels such as "positive" or "negative" are too vague. It's the *finer* points of "sentiment;" e.g. despair, frustration, excitement, curiosity etc. *underneath* the positive or negative sentiment labels we need to get to if we're to understand what's going on with any effect. Notably, to get to this level of sentiment, we need to dig deeper.

Where's the Gold?

We need to dig deeper, but where do we begin? Back to my earlier points about SMM skews/sample issues; we don't know where the *real* gold — vs. fool's gold — lies.

Without spending time and effort to sort through *each and every* "buzzversation" (easily in the thousands), we can't distinguish between content of import and that of little consequence. We just don't know *where* to drill deeper in a meaningful, robust kind of way.

The Verdict

From a *customer service/brand* point of view, quite clearly, SMMs are worth their weight in (real) gold. However, use with caution for your market research. The issues outlined above preclude the output from forming a useful foundation for analysis.

How to Mine Social Media Without Getting Hurt: Listen Carefully to Your Employees and Customers First

Ryan Hanser

Social media is powerful, dynamic and immature, which means attacking the coalface of social media is an easy way to get hurt.

Sure, some still question the power of social media. Gartner says that half the Fortune 1000 will fail in their social media efforts and GfK Roper finds 75 percent of small businesses say they don't know how to use social networks effectively. There is much to learn.

However, anyone engaged in social media directly quickly sees the ways the Internet connects people and markets. Hanser & Associates' work at the coalface has helped fulfill all kinds of client objectives related to customer service, media attention, employee recruitment and more. Social media has delivered immediate, meaningful connections for our clients.

We find the biggest danger is neglecting the power of individuals — employees, customers and other stakeholders — engaged online.

Certainly pushing into groups of people in a monolithic way is a guaranteed path to pain. Moreover, anything that doesn't create value — education, collaboration and so on — is also likely to cause reputational harm. Rest assured that if you're doing something wrong you're going to quickly hear from the irritated people. Also, getting online engagement to scale does take resources; the internet is neither free nor easy. These are lessons better learned by studying the failures of others (and there are plenty!).

Much of our work at the coalface has focused on helping our clients' customers — addressing their issues, incorporating their suggestions, connecting them to each other, promoting genuine opportunities and reinforcing the notion that client organizations are made of people, too.

Those efforts start with listening — a fundamental competency that reinforces safety at the coalface. Listening tools are fast becoming something that can be integrated across organizations, too. They are the foundation upon which organizations can connect to their marketplace in a meaningful way.

And listening is not just for safety's sake. Listening delivers value in allowing customers to help refine products and processes and helping them advocate for our clients. In short, we listen to keep customers engaged in the success of clients.

Indeed, the foundational work on the coalface of social media is to make people — especially customers — happy. Keeping our eyes and ears open and our mouth shut was a prudent beginning. Over time, the opportunities to serve, change and grow have become apparent. That's when the mining begins.

HANSER.com

Social Media Survival: Perpetual Evolution

Claire Grinton

In boardrooms across the world, variation of the same sentiment can be heard: "We need to get on Facebook and Twitter." "We need a mobile app." "We need a Tumblr and a Posterous." In fact, most brands *do* need to consider their presence in social media, and the best ones know to create a strategy unique to their brand and to the medium. But even this level of preparation isn't the end of the story; the best laid plans of mice and men… Well, you know the rest.

The nature of social media is that it is a shared conversation, and we all suffered through enough awkward conversations in middle school to know that preparation is often the easiest part. When it comes down to it, success in social media isn't a product of the strategy, but your ability to evolve and move the conversation forward.

Remember when Skittles tried to use Twitter to aggregate Skittles chatter, only for it to become a huge echo chamber of curse words and porn? It took Skittles only two days to reconsider their approach and replace the homepage with their Facebook fan page instead of the Twitter feed, but ultimately they haven't changed their strategy since the March 1, 2009 launch, putting to rest any momentum they had gained. (When was the last time you went to the site?)

Social media moves in realtime, and brands need to be ready to respond in the same way. As a result, it's imperative to revisit your campaign strategy regularly, with the most frequency upon launch. Put simply, evolution needs to be at the foundation of your strategy:

- On day one of your launch, consider what's working and what isn't.
- On day three, lose any dead weight.
- One week in, be prepared to completely change your tune. Rinse and repeat.

Keep in mind, the role of monitoring and participating in social media is often given to the lowest employee on the totem pole, but they have the greatest insight into your potential for success; listen to what they learn and plan to reconsider your social media strategy with them at regular intervals. Social media campaigns have long legs, and the brands that will make it will be the ones who can keep it engaging, so be proactive, get in the ring, and grow with your consumers.

CLAIREGRINTON.EXTENDR.com

At the Coalface

Marshall Sponder

Social media has inherent limitations — online ***communications are difficult to monitor well*** (*What is the definition of a conversation in social media, anyway?*) and rating conversations for topic/tone/sentiment is both time consuming and not entirely capable of being automated, yet, (*despite claims to the contrary by some vendors*). Measuring conversations are difficult because ***people don't say what they mean***, or don't know — *so how are you or a search engine supposed to?* I found it takes personal involvement to gauge the level, tone and intent of conversation accurately, and managing expectations around a campaign is a vital part of achieving success.

After the strategy part is done, what we've learnt so far is **social media programs** can take anywhere *from 3 months to 1 year to show tangible results,* and you should be measuring changes in your target audience behaviors as ***the fundamental deliverable.*** Social media changed how we communicate and participate in conversation to include audience reactions and participation. One example is the Tamiflu case study, where a blogger, who was also a contender for American Idol, came down with a bad case of the Flu and was ***offered TamiFlu, and blogged about it***. In this case, targeting a person who already had the flu was a highly successful strategy, producing measureable results.

When reaching out to bloggers to elicit conversations, look for, and rate the communities they're part of in descending order, sorting by influence and reach (*first, define the communities you want to engage with*), then measure the contribution the blogger has within that specific community (reach), then rank your influencers based on the contribution. Keep in mind ***every type of communications medium has its own temperature or tone*** and there is a difference in qualitative and quantitative measures of conversation, along with systemic effects (for example, *social media can improve paid search performance by up to 300 percent* according to a Comscore/GroupM study).

Best to think of ***Social Media as a Co-Enzyme, facilitating the Art in Conversations,*** and, if your online conversations support the rest of your business or personal goals, *in ways that are still being quantified,* but whose effects you know and feel in your bones, deep in your gut, tingling your skin, and making life worth living and being part of, you're doing good.

WEBMETRICSGURU.com

Social Media for Business: How to Get It All Done

Caroline Melberg

Once you've decided to put social media to work, having a plan and implementing it well will determine your level of success — and enjoyment — while joining the conversation.

Too often, business owners are lured by the simplicity of social media sites and they jump in without a strategic plan for how social media fits for their business.

Make no mistake — social media offers tremendous benefits to the business owner, but it can also be a huge time waster if it's not implemented with a plan in mind!

While it can seem overwhelming when viewing all your options, here's some tips on getting it all done successfully:

Get Real: Determine Who Will Join the Conversation – if you are a solo entrepreneur, then this one is easy. For businesses with employees, it may not be the CEO or business owner who is best suited to the task. Consider who in your business is best qualified to talk directly to your customers about your products and services in everyday language — not "marketing speak."

Select the Sites to Join: To be successful, social media requires participation and relationships. Just like buying an exercise bike and letting it collect dust doesn't do much to help your figure, there are far too many social media sites online for you to successfully participate in all of them. Visit several sites and find out where people you know are participating. Observe the type of content that is published, and then select three or four social media sites that make sense for the audience you want to reach.

Create a Realistic Schedule: Like any new habit, you need to work social media into your regular routine. An easy way to do this when you're getting started is to block off time in your calendar dedicated to visiting your social media sites and talking with people. Be consistent — but also realistic. Even 15 or 30 minutes consistently is better than an hour scheduled but never acted on.

Don't Forget to Have Fun!: Think of social media for your business like you would a networking event — one that is available any time, and filled with fun people you actually enjoy talking with. Share a bit of your personality, start conversations with interesting people you want to get to know and you'll be surprised how rapidly your following — and your business grows!

MELBERG.com

It's ALL OUR TURF

Eaon Pritchard

Can I just state for the record, RIGHT HERE AND NOW that if I hear Nike+ rolled out one more time as a case study I will literally CHEW MY OWN LEGS OFF and gouge my left eye out with a spoon.

For those working in an agency environment (in which ever of the myriad forms) the reality *at the coalface* is, of course, that in most cases the "average" marketer is the one you're dealing with.

The one who is traditional, arse-covering and risk-averse, FOR THE MOST PART.

This marketer deals in traditional metrics. At best pulled in from search and display — the big problem there is that these metrics don't make any sense in a social "media" context — at worst it's still the largely unmeasureable that's viewed as more effective — the known knowns, if you like.

I recently pitched (to Brand X — a current client) an engagement programme, which would have delivered:

- Connection with a large core group of Brand X's most passionate advocates (PEOPLE)
- Connecting those fans with each other in the brand's space based on shared interest (PASSIONS)
- Created real tangible value around a social behaviour that was already happening (SITUATION)
- Invaluable data from the above and appropriate permission to continue to engage
- Six months of activity where the advocates create and share content with each other
- The ability to leverage that content for SEO purposes as part of an ongoing strategy to reduce dependence on paid search over time
- Something the advocates would 'advertise' (ie viral by nature)
- A permanent activity based asset for the brand to reuse
- The activity was contextual to NPD delivering a reason to buy
- NO MEDIA SPEND (£0) (zilch) (not a fucking sausage)
- All for the same price as the MEDIA ONLY of a one month press ad across half a dozen national titles.

Guess what happened? The client spent the budget on the press ad instead. Here were those press ad metrics, something like 68 percent OTS (of 5.5m) at 2.9. That means 68 percent of the "target audience" (whoever they might be) might "see" the ad about three times in that month.
The problem is not that the client bought a press ad, but that the client bought the press ad INSTEAD.

We have been unable to see the truth, because we have fighting for ten square feet of ground.

OUR DIGITAL SILO, our little piece of turf.

That's CRAP, brothers! The turf is ours by right … because it's ALL OUR TURF.

The impact of social media in marketing can only be measured in the context of contribution to the overall effectiveness of all the interdependent marketing activity

AND IT'S ALL SOCIAL NOW.

This is what you are dealing with, and it's this you need to SELL.

A Fast, True Way for Creating Content

Mark Levy

We want to use social media to contribute to the conversation, connect with others, and change the world. These grand goals can be derailed by a problem, though: we, at times, get stuck for content ideas.

Now I'm no social media guru, but I have been writing for decades. One simple method I use to create content might interest you: I keep an ongoing inventory of fleshed-out observations and stories which I can draw on any time I have a project. Consider doing the same. I'll explain.

For the past few years, I've made it a habit to write regularly. Some of the things I write find their way into books and posts immediately. But much of my writing is done to clarify my thinking. Private writing. It's not meant for publication — at least not right away.

Instead of deleting that writing, I cut it into conceptual chunks and deposit those chunks into documents on my laptop. In my document labeled "Positioning," I put the chunks pertaining to positioning. In my "Messaging" document, I put the chunks dealing with messaging. And so forth. I have a document for every subject I commonly write about.

Each document contains hundreds of stray observations and anecdotes on a single topic. These chunks aren't mere fragments. They're complete thoughts. That's what makes this method work. If I read a chunk even a decade from now, it'd make sense to me. Here's an example from my "Positioning" document:

> Many of us tense up when asked to talk about our business in a sentence or two. But we already know how to do it perfectly. It's like talking about a movie. If someone asked about a movie you saw, you wouldn't recount every scene. You'd pick something distinctive. "It's about a robot that travels back in time to protect its inventor", or "It's the new Daniel Day-Lewis film." Talking about your business is no different.

Now, when a project comes up, I dip into the appropriate document and I'm in chunk heaven. Hundreds to choose from. Sometimes I use one as is. Other times I use one as a thought starter for exploratory writing.

Using this method will help you write faster with fewer headaches. It'll also help you write truer. You'll be using material you had time to think about. It won't be stuff you forced out because you couldn't think of anything better.

LEVYINNOVATION.com

The Conversation Before the Conversation Begins

Steve Kellogg

My new client wanted to revise and update her web site content, so we sat down to talk.

In order to tackle this assignment, I needed a full briefing. But I needed to understand what my client was offering.

What I quickly discovered was that my client wasn't ready to talk. She had not defined her target market, or her services, beyond the vague term "wellness coach."

We discussed how her current site was not achieving its potential and what she wanted to accomplish. She had geared her content to establish herself as a professional providing a wide range of services. While all of the information was relevant, it missed connecting with the reader.

Our discussion was deliberate. The first order was to make sure the target client was clearly identified. Next, we discussed how to frame her services, from two standpoints. First, was to consider the benefits to the client, using descriptive feelings such as youthful, energized, happy, contented, and so on. Next, I wanted to give my client a structure around which she could organize and present her services.

This latter concept is one of taking a "soft" service and turning it into a "product" — making it easier for a client to grasp quickly. Also, it helps to organize thinking, create a system for service delivery and improve client understanding. This is turning an open-ended menu of services into an easily defined program or system. Further, it helps to price and communicate expectations to the buyer.

I'm sure by now you see how these steps create the notion of "brand." Also, an integral part of this process is defining the USP, or unique selling proposition. Simply put, what makes you different from others of the same service providers.

Next, we went over the overall marketing objectives of the site. It's surprising how many websites are developed without consideration of marketing purpose, other than getting some information together. We covered such items as blogging, list building, free newsletters and other potential content drivers.

Our conversation ended with a well-defined outline of targets, objectives and service benefits. I now had the tools needed to create the new content, plus I had the client on the same page, so our working process would go smoothly.

It's interesting how a good conversation helps set the stage for creating communication.

WORDSTOSELL.com

You Don't "Execute" a Conversation, You Steer It

Gautam Ramdurai

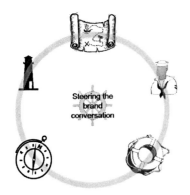

Steering the brand conversation

The decision of striking up a conversation with customers is a lot like traveling on a sailboat. You can calculate the exact location of your destination and chart out a map. You keep on track by using a compass. But you can't control the winds. So, you have to change course dynamically. This needs you to take into account how the winds blow, the tide and, of course, what the compass suggests. Social media strategies are as much about informed execution as they are about sound planning and clear directions.

Keep the Lighthouse Visible

A clear channel of communication between the guys who devise the strategy and the guys who execute the actual campaign. The need for clear direction is greatest when the campaign is already in action.

Which Way Is North?

Constant measurement is key — not just because this is probably one of the few mediums where it is possible but also because of the dynamic nature of the audience and the campaigns themselves. Measurement cannot be an afterthought. It needs to be an integral part of the execution. Measurement helps in constant optimization of strategy and better execution.

Have a Good Map

Define your objectives clearly and set the measurement metrics that are in line with these objectives.

Pick the Right Sailors

Executing a social strategy demands specific abilities. You need to know the platform, know your audience, and understand the objective and the metrics involved. For example, if you assign someone to moderate a forum, they must be better informed about the topic than the audience and should have the ability to steer the conversation.

Lifesavers

Control is one thing you cannot take for granted in this arena. If the winds turn against you and something goes awfully wrong — have a few pre-emptive exit strategies ready — without making it seem like retreat in a battle. For example, Skittles could have used an evacuation plan when their social media campaign got out of control and started harming the brand.

This playing field is new to most of us. The perfect place to fail faster, learn quicker and be agile. Just like it is in sailing, you can't control the winds; but you can make the winds work for you.

GAUTAMRAMDURAI.TUMBLR.com

Closing the Social Media ROI Gap

Jacob Morgan

The first thing we need to do is define what ROI is. ROI is Return on Investment and is calculated as follows: (Gain from investment – Cost of investment) / Cost of investment. ROI is a financial metric, meaning that you're measuring the amount of money that is invested and the amount of money that is returned. Think of high school algebra: what you do to the right side of the equation you must do to the left. This means that if you invest dollars, you can't calculate your return in eyeballs, clicks, website traffic, or anything else that is not dollars. Anything that does not have a dollar sign attached to it is not ROI, it's impact.

Companies need to take a deep breath and relax before jumping into the social media space. Focusing on fragmented three month campaigns that companies have trouble measuring is not the way to go. Instead, companies need focus on implementing an ROI framework that will allow them to measure ROI across all campaigns in both the short term and the long term.

The ROI challenge for organizations can be broken up into two parts: business challenges and technology challenges. Business challenges include everything from understanding things such as the average dollar amount per transaction and customer purchase cycle to making sure that the company executives are all on the same page in terms of understanding what ROI is.

Technology challenges can be vast but include things such as being able to track customers across various online spaces over time to being able to aggregate and make sense of the data that is collected. Companies need to realize that understanding the ROI from social media efforts is going to become imperative. Internal CRM systems, analytics platforms, sales data, and business/customer data all need to talk to each other. Fragmented data sources are going to keep companies from measuring and understanding ROI.

It's also important to note that ROI is just a number which means nothing by itself. The real value comes from understanding the variables that affect ROI so that you can then maximize that number. Developing an ROI framework is not only going to help a company understand the ROI from their social media efforts but it will also help with understanding ROI across all departments.

Just because you couldn't measure the ROI from a billboard doesn't mean you should apply that same mentality to the online space.

JMORGANMARKETING.com

Identities, Friends and Trusted Strangers

I've Got You Under My Web Skin

Armando Alves

In this age of realtime updates, it's easy to misunderstand our closeness to others for the volume of conversations created by the social web. We seldom get to know the real person behind the profile, but only get a glimpse of her web skin, sometimes thick (blog and forum comments), sometimes thin (status updates).

This new kind of skin is used to express our identity to others on the web, and it's mostly based on structured information such as URLs or metadata, made available by the semantic web. These layers are defined not only by us as individuals, but also by the our relationships (represented by reputation and social capital) with the other nodes on our social graphs.

From personal connections to professional acquaintances, we've built our own web skin, with our day-to-day interactions, with small digital footprints regarding hobbies or musical tastes, establishing not only who we are but also how we relate to others.

The newly found web skin has a temporary nature, renewing itself as we change jobs, friends and most importantly, the technology we use. Our volatile digital profiles represent one of the main challenges for the social web — the need to empower individuals to access and control this personal, structured data. As Mozilla's UX chief, Aza Raskin says, "Your identity is too important to be owned by any one company."

Community efforts like DataPortability.org or public APIs (user interfaces to data) are trying to make it easier to share our constructed online identities, not only to other web services but also to the real world. With this effort, they are also becoming a source of valuable offline experiences, with technologies like location based services or near field interaction hard-linking our digital identities to the physical world.

Making our web skin available offline once again requires new discussions about privacy, information filters, data exchange and redefining the concept of ambient intimacy: Do I want my new web skin to be touched by everyone? What kind of mechanisms will be provided to express personality?

As we answer these questions, we'll also be taking huge steps to embed data in the real world, making it easier for individuals, groups and companies to act upon it. Our web skin will become more than a simple picture or nickname — it will carry a huge amount of structured data that can be given huge meaning as we link it to the real world. And then it might achieve one of the ideals of the web — to bring us closer, for real.

ASOURCEOFINSPIRATION.com

Our Future Friends Are Our Objects

Helge Tenno

We still think of digital as something visible, tangible and important. But digital as a concept is rapidly becoming invisible, and as soon as it disappears into people's everyday life there will be no difference between real life and its digital augmentation. When designing marketing strategies for the next two, three or five years we have to take the consequences of this into consideration.

Where we today discuss social media as something additional, a bonus, or even as earned media, conversations in the new marketing landscape will be obligatory. It will be as natural to have a conversation with a company's marketing as it is having one with people in real life.

This requires us to expand our notion of what a conversation is and what marketing is. We need a new mindset.

Marketing is more than just selling products; it's adding value in the context where the product is important, so the company establishes a direct relationship with the participant inside the situation where the product is used or its value meaningful. This gives marketing more the form of services, utilities and arenas than campaigns and display advertising.

A conversation is more than just the exchange of vocabulary language between two or more people. Rather a conversation is a rich exchange of ideas through several languages expressed synchronously and consciously, subconsciously or unconsciously between identities.

What we define as the social web today is not the future of the conversation. The future of the conversation is everywhere, as digital is everywhere and marketing is everywhere. And our future friends are identities, which might as well be people as objects.

180360720.no

Sleeping with Strangers

Andy Drish

It's 6:00 am and I just hopped on a plane destined for Los Angeles.

When I land, I'm meeting Raphael who loves to dance, party, and hang out at fancy night clubs. He's letting me sleep on his couch tonight. Tomorrow I'm crashing with Jesus, who speaks five languages and is studying to be a neurosurgeon. I'm spending my last night chilling with Francesca, who studied abroad with a mutual friend in Japan.

I have never met any of these people.

All I know about them is what I read on their profile at Couchsurfing.com — a website where people open their homes to strangers who are traveling. (Sounds creepy, right?)

Each time I explain Couchsurfing, people are skeptical. How do you know they're not an axe murderer or a serial rapist?

Well … you don't.

So why have over a million people joined the Couchsurfing.com social network?

As the internet evolved, it morphed into a social destination. New technology has encouraged people to become more and more transparent with each other. Because of this, people reveal more information about themselves online than ever before.

And humans naturally trust this transparency. As people become increasingly open online, we become more likely to trust strangers based on their digital identity. Over time, this will make sites like Couchsurfing.com or Airbnb.com much more common.

I've couchsurfed all over the world … Paris, Dublin, Amsterdam. Not to mention a riveting experience in Waterloo, Iowa. Couchsurfing allows people to experience cities from a local's perspective. You spend your time living and breathing the culture of the city instead of wasting time in tourist traps.

Peoples' faith in one another makes all of this possible. This faith will continue to grow as we publish more information about ourselves online. A quick Google search can reveal a person's values, beliefs, personality, friends, and interests through their profiles, blog, and photos. Their entire digital identity is available at the click of a button.

When you know all of that personal information about someone, crashing on their couch seems completely reasonable … Even if you've never met in person before.

Unless, of course, if you find their profile on the National Sex Offender Registry … then, think twice.

ANDYDRISH.com

Is Your Private Life Gone for Good?

Drew McLellan

One of the uncomfortable truths that social media is hoisting upon us is that the clear separation between our personal and professional lives, that the previous generation enjoyed during their careers, is now nothing more than an illusion. If we even try to keep up the facade.

My Facebook friends, Twitter followers and even my LinkedIn account (not to mention all the other social media hot spots) are a blend of my friends, family, marketing peers and clients. Your profiles probably look similar.

When I tweet about my never-ending cough or my daughter's latest role in the school play ... my clients see it. When I have my most recent blog post or a link to a marketing article appear on my Facebook news feed ... my friend, the corporate chef sees it. There's no way to keep the two apart.

Here's what I'm wondering. If someone else employs you — does your employer in essence own a part of your social media persona? Can you ever really have a genuinely private "private life" again?

Aren't your (despite any disclaimer language) words and actions reflecting upon your employer just as much as they do on you the individual when you tweet, blog or update a status?

- Does your boss want you posting weekend party pictures to your Flickr account?
- Should you be playing "Pimp Fight" on Facebook when you know that some of your friends are also clients of your employer?
- Do your blog posts (again, regardless of the disclaimer) reflect on your boss or company as much as on you?
- When you drop an F-bomb in a Tweet, do you think your employer has the right to wince?

The practical truth is that we are now living a blended life. Work doesn't stop when our personal life kicks on and visa versa. So what does that mean?

From the employers' perspective, we're suddenly at huge risk. Every political opinion expressed, every curse word uttered, every off color remark now is tied directly to our company.

From the employees' perspective, we're suddenly stripped of our privacy, unless we opt out of social media. And for many people, based on their generation or profession — that's not an option.

It will be up to us to figure out how to meld this new reality with our existing world ... and our world of the future.

Got some ideas?

DREWSMARKETINGMINUTE.com

Unmasked, Unabashed Identity Transparency

Marilyn Pratt

I'm a grandma and a social activist and an opinionated participant advocate. In short, I'm the antithesis of the expunged, sanitized, "tow-the-party-line" brand emissary one might have expected to find in a corporate-hosted setting. Yet, I hope I represent some of what's very authentic about my company, its listening abilities and its products. That "authenticity" is something that allows real identities of members and administrators to surface and something that fosters the existence of personas that aren't just vapid prototypes and role definitions but a constituency of concrete, three-dimensional, actual and unique individuals, making up a diverse, dynamic and dense community of passionate product users, experts and practitioners in addition to housing and hosting some very vocal and visible critics and critiques.

Welcome to the network of "faced" company reps, product evangelists, brand mentors and named customers and partners. This is a place (as opposed to some other more sterilized, contrived, faceless and anonymous online 'hoods) that hosts forum discussions and wiki spaces and blog posts, where pseudo names are discouraged and personal details and candor are encouraged.

We want to know who you are and even give you a business card, a wiki profile, a blogger author page to fill and draw a picture of yourself and share those artifacts with us and with others. We, in turn, supply our own vitae, flag ourselves as employees or moderators and mentors and even provide a climate to rant, speak beyond product, engage socially, dissent, and schmooze. This is no place for the anemic or for the perceived mindless cheerleaders. You lose your logon ability and become "guestified" or terminated here, if you refuse to be real. Acceptance is based on your willingness to be transparent. No community of ghost writers and panderers. To belong to this tribe you must expose your identity, your experiences and even share a bit of self.

You cannot be faceless on Facebook or disjointed on LinkedIn or under-opinionated in Wordpress or a twit on Twitter. Unmasked, unabashed transparency with a generous admixture of biographic detail is the order of the day in our backyard. Kick our tires and deflate them, but use your own boots and tie your own shoelaces. Mask your true self and your agenda at your risk. Ours is a network of human beings not marketing bots or brand groupies.

WEBLOGS.SDN.SAP.com/pub/u/1915
GRANNIMARI.BLOGSPOT.com

Identities, Friends and Trusted Strangers

B.J. Smith

You hear a knock at your triple-locked front door and peek out through the little peephole. You see me standing there, a handsome devil if I do say, but you don't recognize me.

I shout through the door, "Will you be my friend?"

You might not call 911 right away, but you certainly wouldn't open the door and let me in to rummage around, look through your family pictures and read your diary.

The digital equivalent of talking to strangers is rarely as dangerous as that might be (although I wouldn't hurt a fly, really), but a little discretion in establishing online relationships is a positive thing. Choose your "friends" and share your content as carefully as the context warrants:

- If you're just getting familiar with social media, connect first with family and others who are friends in the non-digital world. Keep most of your information accessible just to friends. Expand as your comfort level grows.
- On a professional network, keep it professional. If you're a pro, you don't need me to explain this.

There's no real rule book, but here are a few ideas you might keep in mind:

- Participate *deliberately* in the online community. In other words, have a purpose. Think carefully about why you're there, whether it's to stay in touch with family and friends, to promote a cause, or build a business.
- You can have more than one purpose, but keep all of them in mind in the digital world, where lines between personal and business blur easily and nothing is really private. Snark about your job in the wrong place and it can cost you.
- If you don't want something to come back and bite you on the ass, don't put it out there. Whatever it is, it will turn up at the worst possible time.
- Don't blog, tweet, comment, pose for pictures or let anyone catch you on video if you're drunk. Ever.
- Angry or otherwise having a bad day? Consider staying away from the keyboard. You don't want to be anti-social in social media.

That's about where the negatives end.

Go forth and explore now. Have fun. Be creative. Discover how your new friends and favorite places can enhance your life, and how you can add something to theirs.

And if we bump into each other somewhere, be sure to introduce yourself. CUOL.

BJSMITH.us

"Never Trust a Stranger," Said My Grandmother (and Kim Wilde, Too)

Véronique Rabuteau

For sure, some of our childhoods have been filled with phrases of warning. Do not accept sweeties from people you don't know in the street, etc. We, as children were afraid of these obscures silhouettes, we, as adults, strongly remember, even if we are more or less conscious of it.

So, what is happening now in the world wide web? Who am I? Am I a stranger to be feared?

In a way, it is exactly the same old story — it is you on Web, not different — even "behind" a computer screen, as it is sometimes underlined.

But two things have mainly changed, and this is very new:

- Our identities will now be shared and stored completely differently; part of them will no more belong to us; it is not a matter of self — sometimes, it is — it is a new, public *representation*. As if you add a line on your business or personal card. Far more too, and we have to think of it, probably with crossed point of views and fields.
- This is a conversational period: which means that you — or your company — can, simply and directly, encounter strangers, that are sometimes your customers — and, *vice versa*, all over the world, mostly in real time. These unknown people will become, for a very few, friends, or trusted strangers — which means, people who will be *reliable*, in a way or another. This means, for example, that you could click on their links without fear of encountering a "bad apple."

You could sometimes even know them far better than "a friend of a friend" in the old fashioned way. When you read, discuss, share and build your connection and relationships online, it takes times but it is also written — and it can be checked by anyone.

Obviously there are some false and fake friends and nobody can be absolutely clear of them. But, with honest use and common good sense, you have nothing to lose, and — maybe — far more to gain.

This is the Age of Conversation, which means an unprecedented way to communicate.

It's not completely *terra incognita*. It's a new way, but not a full tech computer world. It is also a human path.

RABUTEAU.BLOG.OUESTJOB.com

The Who of You

Debra Helwig

Back in the recesses of time, in the days before the internet and digital cameras, I hired a photographer. Not just any photographer, mind you. A wedding photographer. For my Biggest. Day. Ever.

Photoguy was expensive. Exclusive. His references, impeccable.

His work? *Scandalously bad.*

Of course, by the time *we* found out, it was far too late. Holding my dove-eyed, soft-focus photo of *the priest* and other photos equally ludicrous, I wanted to die. Or kill him. Or both. Seventeen years later, I'm still mad.

Could I have prevented this disaster?

Back then, not really. But today, *ahhhh*. Today, I could. I could check his online photo gallery. Read reviews on a dozen opinion sites. Search Facebook or Twitter to see what others say — and read his blog or LinkedIn profile to see what he says for himself. I'd be 100 percent sure of what I was getting before I made the call.

Thank you, social web.

Now, let's think about you for a minute. Yes, *you.*

If you're a stylist, before I place my grown-up-baby-girl in your hands for her prom, do I want to know how well others say you do your up-do voodoo? *You bet.*

If you're a financial planner, do I want to know your track record before I fork over grandma's nest egg? *Oh, yeah.*

If you're a copywriter, will I care that your missed deadlines cost more than one business a critical opportunity? *Indeedy.*

And on and on.

In your job (no matter what your job), you are the architect of others' life-defining moments, whether you know it or not. That means people like me want to be certain *you're* the one we can trust.

So, tell us.

When you blog or tweet, post to Facebook or join a group on LinkedIn, you give the world an inside look at the *Who of You.* Anything you write, anything you share, who you hang with online — it all tells people about how you roll. Why you're worthy.

Suddenly, your credibility is visible 24x7x365. All people have to do is read, and they'll know you deserve their time — and their business.

People like me — clients and customers — are waiting for reasons to trust you. Why don't you get social and show us?

Because the Who of You is a beautiful thing, but we only know it if you share.

Interesting Is the New Bland

Emily Reed

I started my first blog while schlepping a heavy laptop across Europe with my new Australian boyfriend. I wanted to practice writing and had every intention of capturing our fights, mushy declarations of love or any other embarrassing details along the way. After all, that's what I love in other writers — the bravery to push for deeper truth and reveal the intimate.

Thanks to matching sinus headaches, I didn't have to wait long for juicy content in the form of jetlag inspired bickering (dialogue!). But just as I was finishing my first post, he casually mentions that his parents would be reading as we go. His *parents* — who I hadn't met yet and who were expecting us for Christmas at the end of the trip.

Ack! Backspace, backspace, backspace.

In one fell swoop, my online identity went from Carrie Bradshaw to Lonely Planet Europe.

I can't tell you how thankful I am that it wasn't as, erm, interesting as I had planned it to be. Because they create conversations, there's a certain basic level of public-ness that applies to all of the social media (plus, his parents are now my in-laws).

But I made the mistake that many brands make — I went generic; I went boring.

Instead of thinking of it as writing, I switched to thinking of it as chat, say, at a dinner party. And while some people are wonderful entertainers in those situations, I myself am more of a listener/responder. Saying little supportive things that only the speaker really appreciates. (In this mode, for example, I adore Facebook's "Comment" and "Like" buttons.)

But the bloggers and Twitterers and brands that I love *do* push the comfort zone. They say things that are surprising and controversial and personal. They apply the basics of good writing to the genre.

So I'm forever bouncing in my mind between asking myself, "is this good, interesting writing?" and "Would I be embarrassed if my clients or in-laws were reading this in front of me right now?" If the answer is "yes" to the first question, I move to the second. If the answer to the second is "yes," I hit the "save as draft" button and wait a day. Ninety percent of the time, I've gotten over myself enough to remember that, as long as I remember the public-ness, being part of the conversation is also about entertaining my fellow dinner guests.

CONFORMISTSUNITE.com

Where Is the Outrage?

George Jenkins

Everyone who has used the internet today, has probably experienced websites that:

- Present Privacy and Terms of Conditions policies that regularly state they collect consumers' personal data and share it with other companies — affiliates and partners — but don't disclose those companies' names
- Notify you when third-party applications use your personal data, but fail to disclose exactly which personal data items the application will store and share with other companies. Nor does the notification name those companies (Facebook.com is famous for all of this)
- Use cookies technology immediately on the home page to identify and track its website visitors' usage, before you've had a chance to read the website's Privacy and Terms policies
- Employ advertising programs that track consumers' web usage across several websites
- Make money collecting and reselling your personal information. We've all heard of Equifax, Experian, and TransUnion — but rarely hear about the 100+ other regional, smaller credit agencies.

Are we consumers so addicted to websites that offer free services, news, and applications that we no longer care what these companies do with our personal information?

Are we consumers so addicted to convenience — fast credit, quick and easy purchases — that we no longer care what companies do with our personal information?

Have we consumers just given up — stopped fighting — to maintain control of our sensitive personal data?

Or are we consumers just happy being relatively uninformed shoppers that ignore websites' privacy and terms of use policies?

Where is the outrage by consumers?

IVEBEENMUGGED.TYPEPAD.com

Living Authentically in a Transparent World

Michelle Beckham-Corbin

We live our lives today pressed between the flowing pages of Twitter and the back and forth banter of blogs. We connect with professionals via their profiles on LinkedIn and run them through Google search as a matter of routine background check. Presented with rich content, we sift through the information trying to determine our desired level of connection.

The tentacles of our personal brand are out there on the social media highway, reaching out and touching each person who zips by. We try hard to be engaging and hope that the hook we thrust out is the one that will spear them and bring them front and center to the hub of our existence; the place where we make the sale.

This can't happen without taking the conversation to a deeper place where we can become intimately connected to each other. How we get there is a matter of trust and is a crucial point in establishing lasting relationships. Those who have presented themselves in an authentic way online will appear seamlessly the same in person, while others who have experimented with online personas that don't truly represent who they are will find continued relationships lacking as "purchasers" of our brand discover the existing holes.

In 2004 I stumbled onto the infant social media highway and learned these lessons in a very unusual way. Concerned about a very popular fantasy MMORPG game that my ten year old son was obsessed with, I created an account, got hooked on the game and went on to become one of the highest ranking female players . I chronicled my experiences in a series of essays backed up with research on the emerging social media tools that the players were integrating into their gaming. I found the research enlightening and began to incorporate social media into my personal life and later into my corporate marketing work. It was here that I truly learned the importance of being authentic and balancing transparency with trust.

I left the fantasy game world long ago and exist now on multiple social media platforms that reflect my company and personal brand. I have developed virtual business relationships through Twitter, LinkedIn and Facebook which have led to meaningful collaboration offline. Trust will always be an inherent part of taking the next step, but it is a developed risk needed to arrive at a deeper level of doing business.

CREATINGCONNECTIONSCONSULTING.com

Identities, Friends and Trusted Strangers

James Stevens

Talking at TED about "how social media can make history" in June 2009, Clay Shirky stated, "These tools don't get socially interesting until they get technologically boring."

That's what's happened to the web. It's always had the ability to be social — forums, anyone? But only when the likes of Facebook et al became the norm (that is, boring), did the social stuff really start to take off.

And it's had a dramatic impact on the way humans interact. Not only can we stay in touch with friends and family more easily, but professional contacts too —past, present and future.

Ultimately, this has to make us think differently about our identity. It's no longer "professional *or* personal." It's not "public *or* private." It's both. Together.

When Kimberly Swann started her new office job in Essex, England on February 2. 2009, she was soon bored by the menial tasks given to her. She didn't moan to friends in person, though. She posted thoughts on her Facebook page. Three weeks later, with her boss having discovered the comments, she was sacked: see BBC news: http://is.gd/4VHQ4.

Kimberly compartmentalized her identity. Work was work and the web was personal. And, before this social lark really took off, you *could* make a distinction in your life.

But that time has now gone. Today, everyone's online and getting social. Colleagues and friends. All mixed up together.

The result? Your online identity is no longer your identity online. It's your identity. We now have to portray ourselves online as we would in real life. Because the social web has caught up with the real world. Lives online are now as rich a social tapestry as they are offline.

It's always been sound advice when someone says "be yourself." But that advice has never been so relevant in today's uber-connected world. Just because our professional and private lives are coming together online more than ever before doesn't mean you need to act like someone else. Rather, it's more important than ever to act exactly as you would do. Because this isn't a new restriction. It's an opportunity. To show just how great you really are to *everyone*.

BREATHINGSINCE1978.WORDPRESS.com

Who Are You?

Brendan Tripp

Despite becoming increasingly "multimedia," the internet is, at core, a text medium, and there has always been an undercurrent of "veiled identity" in the written word. From such notable antecedents as Benjamin Franklin (who wrote as "Richard Saunders" in his famed *Almanacs*), generating writing that one prefers to not have specifically linked to oneself has a long tradition. It is no surprise that, as technology evolved and produced the internet, the web, and the current explosion of social media, the temptation to "be somebody else" is still quite strong.

From the earliest days of IRC and "chat rooms," there was always a question as to the real identity of people on the other end of the modem line. The anonymity of the digital connection allowed a wide range of behaviors, from the sleazy misrepresentation of age and gender aimed at taking advantage of the unwary, to the ability to "troll" extreme views in the pursuit of conflict-induced adrenaline rushes. It also, of course, enabled a vast reach across the planet, providing a means for like-minded individuals to connect with each other without limitations of geographic proximity.

However, in a world increasingly electronically linked, it's becoming less easy to be an anonymous voice, and individuals are now facing serious choices of how they present themselves in the digital environment. While one may be unable to defend against the embarrassing cell phone picture appearing, most users have to grapple with their own personal presentation on the web. Do you separate your personal and professional life? Do you "keep your family out of it"? Do you create "personas" for various purposes, or "compartmentalize" politics, religion, and sexuality? All of these carry potential complications with work, community, and one's immediate circle of contacts, and nearly everybody has to find their own way through that minefield.

It is the rare individual who consciously stakes out a fully-rendered "me" online, given the conflicts possible, yet it is also the uncommon individual who will only discuss particular subjects when appearing as a specific identity, leaving a large grey area in between. While a certain amount of discretion is certainly called for, one does need to step back from time to time and ask "Who am I?" within the digital context, and try to make that entity as substantial as the analog person behind it.

BTRIPP.NING.com

The Stories Customers Tell: 4 Ways to Boost Your Positive Online Buzz

Casey Hibbard

You're close to fulfilling a lifelong dream — visiting Peru's lost city of Machu Picchu.

For years, you've squirreled away a little of every pay check just for this adventure. Decisions about tour companies, sights and lodging can be the difference between an average vacation and the trip of a lifetime.

But you don't personally know anyone who has gone before. Where do you turn?

To strangers. Or rather, strangers with experience.

Whether that big purchase or decision is about a dream vacation, a financial planner, or enterprise software, the stakes are high.

To reduce perceived risk, today's buyers look to the experiences of others — increasingly documented online on forums, blogs, discussion groups, vendor websites, Twitter, and other social media sites.

Hopefully, your customers are saying good things about you.

No matter what you're selling, here are four ideas for elevating your *positive* online buzz:

1. **Capture your own stories** — Feature your happy customers in written, video or audio stories. Just don't make it all about you. Make it about the customer's experience. Then post those success stories on your website, blog, Twitter, Facebook and other relevant sites.

2. **Turn frowns upside down** — Proactive companies track mentions of them online. When it's positive, thank customers. If not, respond and make it right. Those customers are then more likely to counter with a positive mention about your proactive response.

3. **Ask for reviews** — When a happy customer tells you such, encourage her to share her experiences on relevant sites. Today, there are online customer feedback sites for everything from travel to CRM software to cameras.

4. **Hold a contest** — Often, your best customers want to share their stories, and in doing so, they look good too.

Run a creative contest where customers submit their top stories related to your product or service, and then showcase the winners online.

Make a habit of capturing, telling and repurposing your customers' positive experiences every chance you get. The payback — prospects will find those stories and gain confidence in choosing you.

STORIESTHATSELLGUIDE.com/blog

Banking On Trust and Social Capital

Jenny Meade and David Svet

In the early 1990s a bank in the USA's north-east with over 200 branches conducted some research on "this internet thing." Did they really need to offer online banking to stay competitive? They didn't believe they could do it without compromising their systems — a terrifying risk. How could they trust their customers and employees with direct access to their systems from home? Then they found a study that said only 7 percent of US households had a PC. They waited.

Meanwhile, a community bank in North Carolina with 25 branches was providing free online banking. They used a proprietary system they had paid dearly for and for several years were the only bank in the area that offered such a thing. They grew exponentially.

Now social media has made the internet a giant party where everyone is connected. There are no borders, barriers, or boundaries. We share our lives in realtime making friends from strangers all over the world. Even business is social. It seems every brand has a social media presence staffed by hyper connected internet mavens who lavish friendly service on their adoring customers. Everyone is important. Everyone has an opinion. Everyone is there to help — everyone except most of the banks. They are afraid. There's too much risk. How could they trust their employees to talk with customers through social media?

Social networks are based on trust and relationships — just like banks. We build social capital every time we help someone, whether it's online or in person. Social capital is a core driver of business success. It always has been, but now the barriers to creating it are gone. We can meet people online anywhere, anytime. But they're strangers. You have to get to know them to become a friend, to gain their trust. It's still requires human interaction, the only part that's changed is the communication channel.

The early adopters are getting the first shot at a massive opportunity. To not be there is to choose to die alone. Meanwhile, in a boardroom somewhere near you, an executive team is deciding to block access to social media. Yet, they each have an internet capable phone in their pocket, as do most of their employees. The fortress they think they are protecting is gone, but nothing has been breeched except the trust between employer and employee while a competitor eats their lunch.

LINKEDIN.com/in/jennymeade
SPURCOMMUNICATIONS.com

Accepted Realities

Joanne Austin-Olsen

My first experience of virtual reality was a Tomorrow's World demonstration featuring people in sci-fi goggles wandering around a futuristic, linear landscape. It was rubbish. Thankfully, the virtual reality we have now is an online world that reflects ours, is widely populated and is actually pretty good. In fact, this online "accepted reality" is often more real to us than the world we live in (our "actual reality").

I'm not asserting that we literally live in dark rooms staring at screens and communicating with our thumbs. I'm talking about our identities in accepted reality. They are creations, yes, but often more accurate than fictional.

Your accepted personality may reflect how you see yourself, want to be seen, are seen by others. It's irrelevant. What matters is that it invariably highlights those aspects of yourself (and your behaviour) that motivate you and by which you've actively chosen to define yourself.

This self-definition exposes as arrogant and hopelessly outdated the received assumption that we (as communicators) can impose broad definitions on societal groups. Arguably, looking at someone's hash tags is more illuminating than looking at their occupation or status. Demographics be damned — accepted reality is an egalitarian place to live.

We're also startlingly willing to share personal information here — photographs, intimate moments, secret thoughts. When we walk here, we tend to walk naked. This self-exposure is at the heart of the dichotomy defining accepted reality — the more we share, the more fiercely we protect our privacy. The more we give, the less others are permitted to take. Here, relationships are reciprocal.

These rules of engagement apply to accepted friends, actual friends and brands alike. The actual reality differentiation between person-person relationships and person-brand relationships doesn't exist. This brings with it a redefinition of responsibility and a significantly higher sensitivity to unwanted versus wanted conversation. There's no difference between an old school acquaintance pestering you to rekindle a non-existent friendship and a brand approaching you with targeted messages because accepted reality has led it to believe it 'knows' you. Both will be rejected (or "unaccepted").

It's simple to build a successful and connected place for yourself here. Exhibit characteristics and behaviors that are likeable, that will encourage people to respond to you. They will seek you out and, ultimately, befriend you. After all, whether we're looking into each others' actual eyes or virtual ones, some things don't change.

THEINCREDIBLESHRINKINGWOMAN.WORDPRESS.com

The Dual Life of the Flaneur

Gavin Heaton

When we step out into the digital landscape, we make a decision to embark on a journey from whose grasp we may never return. It's an experience that, for many of us, is both expected and surprising — ultra modern, yet strangely familiar. We are — in the instant — what Baudelaire would call "a passionate spectator" — observer and observed, anonymous in the face of the crowd — yet keenly signalling our identity one @ symbol at a time. This is the dual life of the digital flaneur.

For the first timer — the virgin participant — the crowd can overwhelm with its infinite sameness. One face, one quip repeated *ad nauseum* echoes across our screens devoid of grace — and can be easily discounted. But for the digitial flaneur, this is an invitation as inevitable as the tide. Tingling, she enters the vast reservoir of humanity and is enveloped by its stream of consciousness — connected and connecting, acting and being acted upon.

The transition we have seen over the last decade on the web, from static or even database driven content to social, pluralistic, real time conversations is marked not by its wavelength but by its amplitude. The digital flaneur is not interested in the spread of ideas but in their relevance. She seeks not the voices of many but the conversations of the passionate. This journey carries its destination in the heart of its interactions not in its logical end point.

But who is this digital flaneur?

Remarkably, the social technologies which are connecting and engaging us all — the young and the old, the smart, the wise, the beautiful and the ignorant — are reigniting and satisfying an almost forgotten human impulse: curiosity. Better yet, participation itself creates identity — we are what we do, what we say, what we write and how we behave. We are our reputation.

To call the digital flaneur a "jack of all trades" would be to mistake her intention. While the claw marks of history pock the buildings of our deserted metropolises, the digital flaneur steps willingly into the torrent of other people's lives. She participates in the living history of individuals, distilling moments of eternity from the minutiae of our everyday lives. Sometimes she shares, sometimes she conscientiously objects. Her optimism is abundant, her rally call the hashtag.

But she's no longer sitting at home — isolated, forlorn. She's on the street, outside your window. She waits at the bus stop by you. She's the private professional outside your corner suite. The digital flaneur for all of us, the future and the past.

SERVANTOFCHAOS.com

41

Conversation Quotient: Truthfulness + Usefulness

Angela Maiers

One of the things I teach is Reading With the Writer in Mind. Noting and valuing that reading on the web can sometimes be silent conversations between writer and reader, the habit of thinking about the writer is a non-negotiable. Not just whether the writer is truthful, but whether what they are saying is useful.

Truthful

In a time where conversations, connections, and collaborations are becoming available in many ways (i.e.,speed, reach, ubiquity) we should be addressing appropriateness of use. Our own and our kids.

But hasn't it always been so? I remember being taught life lessons of how to behave in public and in private. By those lessons, I became equipped to tell who was authentic and consistent when meeting people. The more social engagement on my part, the stronger my discernment muscles grew.

When in front of our computers or mobile devices, it becomes too easy to forget there are human beings on the other side. And the electronic tools are connective tools, not masks.

On the social web, there can be valuable findings in our "first impressions" of a web page or social media profile, just as with "first-impressions" when meeting someone in person. Here's the criteria I recommend:

- Is there a real person here? Look for a face (not a cartoon) a name (not a pseudonym)
- Can I contact them? A phone number or email address?
- When was their last update? Consistency and Frequency breeds Authenticity
- Do others link to them (Google Blog Search and the URL or BackTweets.com)
- Is their communication filled with adverts and pitches?

These five questions can usually be answered in a matter of seconds and above the scroll line.

Usefulness

Evaluating for truthfulness is important, but so is usefulness. Even if the author is truthful and authentic, each reader must decide whether the content and conversation is Nice to Know vs Need to Know.

The questions I ask myself to determine usefulness:

- Can I apply what I learn?
- Can I share what I learn?
- Can I modify or combine what I learn?

The Conversation Quotient of Truthfulness + Usefulness allows us as readers to quickly determine which pieces of information we engage with, saving us headaches and time, while making us smarter quicker.

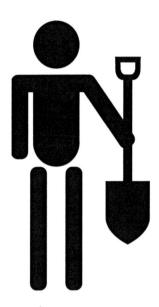

Conversational Branding

Conversational Branding — Almost as Easy as Breathing But Without the Risk of Inhaling a Bug

Tim Jackson

In this new age of conversation, what many of us know of "branding" (or assume we know) has morphed into something that is a far cry from the traditional definition of *"the use of logos, symbols, or product design to promote consumer awareness of goods and*(or) *services."*

Branding now has less to do with creating an image or idea of your company and putting it out into the world for people to look at and leave alone. Today, branding has everything to do with how well and to what extent we reach out and engage the people who are interacting with our brands. It's no longer possible to simply bait the hook and wait for the bite. If anything, we have to get into the water and swim with the fishes!

As brands, it is hard (if not impossible) to be everywhere at once and engage in all possible conversations at the same time, but don't let that scare you away from trying. It's much easier than you might think to have an effective and relevant impact on the conversations taking place about us and our brands. Simply creating a Twitter account or Facebook page isn't quite enough, but it is a start.

Once you've taken the plunge and created a blog, or Facebook/ Twitter account, the real works begins, but it is far less frightening than you think. In fact, it is so intuitive you might just find that you even *enjoy* it!

Here are 3 simple tips that will help get you started;

1. Once your community finds you, go find them — reaching out and replying to a comment or saying thanks for a link to your site or a re-tweet gains you tons of appreciation.

2. Don't be afraid to be you and speak in your own voice — it's ok to be conversational, as if you were simply talking to your friends or family. In fact, it goes a long way toward humanizing who you are and what you do.

3. Ask questions — nothing builds investment or "pride of ownership" faster than asking people what they think. You'll be amazed at how fast people will tell you how much they'd like to give you their money for listening.

It really is very simple, as well as effective — and might just prove to be something you really enjoy too! The conversation is out there — be a part of it.

MASIGUY.com

New Age of Farming

Chris Wilson

It's time for us to become farmers. No I'm not talking about trading in your laptop and smartphone for a tractor and heavy harvesting machinery. I'm talking about a different type of farmer, one that grows brands organically.

For over 50 years, commercial brands were built through a structured, almost mechanical planning process. This method depended heavily on the use of mass media and advertising to build up brands in the minds of consumers, who depended on mass media and advertising to keep them informed on everything from national news to what kind of cereal to buy. This provided organizations with a high level of control over what their brands looked like and how the public perceived them. With the right visual appeal, a well-constructed communication message, a mediocre product or service, and enough cash, a brand could be built with the same precision as a car traveling down an assembly line.

Times have changed. Consumers aren't tethered to advertising and mass media for information anymore. It's literally at their fingertips, with the combination of search and smartphone technology, consumers can now push a single button to access unlimited information about brands, whenever and wherever they want to. This access is uncontrolled by the brand itself, and is driven by raw and unfiltered consumer actions through reviews, opinions and conversations.

In response, a new method of branding is emerging that relies less on structure and control of the brand. This method finds ways to enable the organic growth of the brand by empowering and collaborating with consumers.

Organizations aren't in complete control of their brands anymore, but this doesn't mean that they have to hand everything over to consumer control. There are great opportunities for brands that quit fighting change and find ways to create and lead consumers to content and conversations of value.

The truth of the matter is that organizations can't lead if they continue to take on the role of brand builders. The control they once had as builders just doesn't exist anymore. This means that the only option for organizations wanting to move their brands forward is to accept a role as facilitator of conversations. The organizations that embrace this new role will access opportunities to lead and shape conversations around the brand and connect with consumers in ways that were never possible when brands were built.

Embracing the organic nature of growing a brand provides a lot of benefits to an organization:

- Access to gain continuous insights while interacting with consumers
- Build and nurture long term relationships with consumers
- Supplies consumers with new ways to experience the brand, in some cases, experiences consumers design for themselves
- Keeps the brand agile, involved and connected with the market it serves
- Gives the organization a gauge for where the brand is and where it is going.

The shift from builder to farmer can be a big leap for most organizations but just as it takes a lot of time and tender care to produce a high-yielding agricultural crop, so does growing a brand. It's time to put down the construction gear and start planting seeds.

The Birth of an Online Brand Community

Gaurav Mishra

Once upon a time, a young brand manager named Ria, who was the custodian of a big packaged food brand in a large Indian conglomerate, decided that she was tired of marketing-as-usual.

One typical Sunday evening, as Ria alternated between channel surfing (to avoid inane TV ads) and navigating the Nike+ community (to compare her last month's running stats with her friend Nikita's), she had an epiphany. She realized that she had a split personality. As a brand manager, she was intent on finding innovative ways to interrupt the lives of her consumers. As a consumer, she was intent on avoiding all types of ads, in print, on TV, and on the web.

Ria was frustrated that even though she spent more money each year on full-page newspaper ads and 60-second television commercials, she could see no evidence that her consumers felt connected with the brand.

Ria knew that if she wanted to connect with her consumers on a one-to-one basis, she needed to engage them around a big social object — a lifestyle, passion or cause — like Sunsilk's Gang of Girls (sunsilkgangofgirls.com) community and Tata Tea's Jaago Re (jaagore.com) voter registration campaign.

Ria decided to build a community for young mothers, who influenced the eating habits of the entire family. The community would not only enable young mothers to connect with each other around concerns that preoccupied them, but also allow Ria to get first hand insights into these preoccupations and their attitudes towards packaged food.

It wasn't an easy sell inside the company. "The internet is really small in India compared to TV and newspapers," her advertising agency argued. "Are you sure that you want to build a brand community, when few of them have become big?" her boss asked.

Ria argued that India's 30 million active internet users are not only young, urban and upwardly mobile, but are also heavy users of social networking and blogging platforms. Add to that India's 400 million mobile subscribers, out of which 20 million-use group SMSing services and 20 million use mobile internet, and the base is big enough to be interesting to most marketers.

Ria knew that few brand communities had become big in India, but felt that it was a reflection of limited vision and not limited potential. Her own experiences with the international Nike+ (nikeplus.com) and Dell Ideastorm (ideastorm.com) communities had shown her the power of a fully realized brand community.

In the end, Ria's passion prevailed. Nine months after she had her epiphany, a new online brand community for young mothers in India was born.

GAURAVONOMICS.com

Brand Interactions Not Included

Dan Schawbel
||||||||||||||||||||||||||||||||||

Most brands have social network accounts right now, but very few have earned their medals as companies that "get it." They may obtain some press in the mainstream media and in blogs, but that will soon end because participating in the social world is mandatory. The reality today is that just having many social networking accounts isn't enough because anyone can register them, with almost no effort. Now brands are being forced to engage at a rate never seen before. For instance, a recent Cone study reported that almost 80 percent of new media users interact with companies or brands through social media sites and tools, which was an increase of 32 percent from 2008! What's even more interesting is that 95 percent of new media users believe companies should have a presence online. The days of sitting back and watching other companies join the conversation are over.

Now the question is "how should they get involved?" Well first, brands have to think about an objective and the desired results they want to achieve. Possible outcomes could be in revenue numbers, brand mentions and overall awareness, list building, etc. Without fully understanding your business objectives, you are wasting time without having anything to measure against. Once you nail the objective(s), then it's time to locate the right people in your organization to seize control of your social media assets, which may include a blog, social accounts and the strategy, depending on the organizational structure and company culture. Finding the right people can be more difficult in larger companies, although you'd have more to choose from. Of course, every employee should support your efforts to promote by retweeting and posting on Facebook, which has no additional costs. You need passionate employees who are experts in their fields to take the lead because they will be able to contribute value to customers and potential customers.

Once you line up the right group of social media supporters, then you need to enable them and empower them because that's what social media is all about. They have to feel like they can interact with stakeholders and help people out, while having access to social accounts to let them do so. Have these brand evangelists start interacting by following people, answering product questions and giving advice. After a while, you will start to see a community formed and then it's what you do with that community that makes all the difference!

||||||||||||||||||||||||||||||||||||||||||||||||||||||||||||||||||||||||||||||||||||||
PERSONALBRANDINGBLOG.com

Your Network Is Your Brand

Dr. Ed Brenegar

Used to be — "It's not what you know, but who you know that counts."
Now — "It's not who you know, but who is talking with you that counts."

Traditionally, a brand is an idea that describes who we are and our products, our companies or organizations. Communicating a brand identity is now more difficult. Everyone has a message to deliver. The number and diversity of tools for reaching potential customers makes it harder to be heard over the noise of so many competing messages.

In the age of conversation, our network becomes our brand.

Our network does not become our brand because we use social media tools, like weblogs, Facebook, LinkedIn, Ning and Twitter. From this perspective, social media is no different than using print and broadcast advertising to get our message out. Today, even the most compelling brand message does not create a branded network. Engaging people in conversation does.

Talking with people about who they are, what they stand for and the value that we can bring to their lives and work is how we create this network. Social media tools enable us to build mutual trust. The character of our relationship with people is the source of the credibility for our brand. They have confidence in us and trust our competency to be who our brand identity says we are.

There are three conditions for turning our network into our brand.

Mission and Values
Clarity about what we stand for and who we are is the foundation. A clear mission and values are the connecting ideas that build our network and our brand.

Open and Collaborative
Being open and collaborative with the people invites people to be a part of our network. We talk with them, not at them.

Strategic Purpose
Having a strategic purpose for social media tools focuses our resources on the impact of our branded conversation. Our network becomes our branded messenger, and we, the facilitators of their efforts.

Turning our network into our brand starts with a change of perception. Our focus shifts from our brand idea to the conversation about why our brand matters. People become integral to creating our brand. Our interaction with people makes the difference, and our impact grows. Who we know, and who is talking with us now our branding activity.

EDBRENEGAR.TYPEPAD.com

The Rise of Digital Personalities: Brands Become Human, and People Become Brands

Hajj Flemings

Corporate brands can no longer afford to just be the 400lb gorilla in the room. They now have to operate as a group of connected people that are engaging and touching their customers realtime. The social web has changed the way we view brands and the way they view themselves, forcing them to act more like humans. Words such as conversation, personality, value, DNA, and relationship are being associated with our favorite brands.

The new voices of corporate brands are not just the people at the top but the people in customer service and those who use social media. Who would have thought Richard Binhammer (aka @RichardatDell) would be one of the most popular voices of Dell versus the founder and owner, Michael Dell? Who would have thought Scott Monty's (@ScottMonty) online work would be just as instrumental in helping to save the Ford Motor Company as Alan Mulally in the mist of the economic downturn in the automotive industry?

Digital Personalities

Digital personalities are personal brands that can operate as brand ambassadors internally and externally for corporate brands.

- *Internally* — Scott Monty (Ford Motor Company) and Frank Eliason (Comcast) are employees who influence the online conversation and engagement of their respective companies
- *Externally* — Gary Vaynerchuk (Wine Library TV) runs various companies and influences the conversation and engagement around wine and other topics that he is passionate about.

The value of digital personalities is increasing daily. Companies are using these personalities to build communities in channels relevant to their target market. Social networks, such as Twitter and Facebook, are great channels for peer-to-peer conversations to reshape the way consumers purchase products, make decisions and ultimately live their lives.

The State of Digital Personalities

People "Friend" Brands — Forty percent of people "friend" brands on Facebook.

Peer-to-Peer Influence — People don't trust advertisements or corporate blogs, but they trust their peers.

Social Media Policies — There will be an increased need for social media policies to establish guidelines for proper protocol.

The rise of digital personalities, internally and externally, is creating new opportunities and innovative ways to humanize brands online. Companies will need connected digital personalities more than ever in the 21st Century.

HAJJFLEMINGS.com/blog

What Do Your Online Conversations Say About Your Brand?

Gordon Whitehead

If one thing has changed during the last few years in social networking, it is the incredible rise in the level of brands holding conversations online. Today brand messages are coming at you from every direction and from every part of the globe.

But in this social networking age how can marketers best differentiate your brand, or brands, in the mind of your prospect by conversing online? And how can you manage and exploit it?

Even if your company is doing well, you just can't ignore it. Your brand reputation and personality is already being fashioned by people within your company and outside your company. It's critical that marketers decide who is best equipped within your company to engage people and what those conversations need to say about your brand.

How do you do this? Well, one of the best suggestions I've heard is detailed in a Forrester report, recommending a fundamental marketing organizational change from having "brand managers" to having "brand advocates." *Advocates* have the freedom and flexibility to respond to conversations online without the ridged constraints of managers or even worse, company lawyers.

Brands are like people — they have *a unique* personality. Brands have to earn trust and respect — if not a brand may end up sounding cheap, or come across as uncaring. As I'm sure you know, people can spread good or bad information about your brand faster than any marketer.

Marketers must ask themselves how to best reconcile offline and online brand personality and image.

Marketers have to take your brand back to the drawing board and start to think through what your brand is supposed to mean offline as well as online. Traditionally, brand personalities were built around traits such as beliefs, values, prejudices, interests and heritage.

However, online conversations give your brand a great opportunity to put together a more complex human personality *allowing* you to differentiate your brand in the same way people shape relationships with other people.

In the end, while many people talk of social networking, few truly understand it, *appreciate* the opportunities it presents or *recognize* the risks associated with doing it *incorrectly* or ignoring it. Brand personalities are shaped and enhanced by joining the online conversation. You won't want to miss out.

THEGIT.com.au

Everyone Loves a Good Story

Scott Townsend

Companies are stories. And customers are looking to be a part of a good story every day. We will part with our hard-earned money in exchange for the opportunity to feel special and for the right to say "we belong." So how do you find your unique story?

Through research and discovery, you can start to piece together your company's history with information such as how the company started, who started it, what obstacles were overcome, etc. When you start putting these pieces together, you get a feel for what the company stands for … and you begin to see the formation of the brand.

With a grasp of your historical self, you now have a story to tell. How do you tell that story? Here are a couple of things to consider:

1. Improve your storytelling ability — read about other companies and see how they tell their story. Several companies that do a good job telling their story are The Walt Disney Co, Hewlett-Packard and Amazon. Start writing a journal and practice putting together small stories about home, work and life.
2. Improve telling your company's story — if you have a company blog, start writing compelling stories about your business that your readers would enjoy. Join Toastmasters to hone your presentation skills. Take the opportunity to speak to local and civic organizations to put your storytelling skills to work.
3. Use visual cues and units of measure to help the customer quantify your story and their experience with your company. For example, United Linen and Uniform Services started in 1936. But what does that tell you? Not much. So we came up with some interesting facts surrounding that date … the Hoover Dam was completed, *Mr. Smith Goes to Town* won the Academy Award for Best Picture, Margaret Mitchell finished *Gone With The Wind* and FDR won a landslide election for his second term as President in 1936. Watch any Ken Burns documentary (*The Civil War, Baseball, Jazz*) to see an expert take facts, figures and a few black and white photographs to help you make an emotional connection to the story he is telling.

Interestingly enough, your company's story does not stop with yesterday's ribbon cutting. The company's story and the customer's perception of the company (your brand) continue to be shaped with each transaction/interaction your customer has with your company.

CREATINGCONTENT.BLOGSPOT.com

Everything Flows — How Traditional Media Decline Offers Opportunities for Brands

Jeroen Verkroost

Traditional media's editorial teams have long functioned as guides and trailblazers for the masses. Newspapers, magazines and TV told people what to do, what to like, what to think. Today consumer emancipation is on the rise, while the power of traditional media's editors is waning. In this continuum, chances abound for marketers and their brands to help fill that void.

But not by claiming this space to insert a product related message. That would not be very sophisticated and it will not be accepted by today's media savvy consumers. The impact would probably be negative, and the chance of a repeat would be minimal.

Instead, smart can brands "earn" their position in the social media space by adopting a topic that fits the brand, and creating a unique environment around this subject. This way the brand can venture into online conversation by offering a destination, an advertiser funded environment that is relevant while it leverages the strength of its visitors to add value.

To do this, make sure that the subject is the theme, but the visitor is the focal point. Build a place that revolves around your guests. Create an attractive platform where the dialogue between consumers on the chosen subject is facilitated, with the brand as the host of the environment.

In essence, this is very much like throwing a party. Like any good host, connect the people that came to you and help them to enjoy what's on offer, as well as each other's company and knowledge. Don't try to force your message in, but make sure that there is a persistent brand presence in the surroundings, and soon your environment will grow, together with the brand connection.

Everything flows, and wherever there is movement, space is created.

Marketer, jump in – it's time to get busy!

COPYPASTE.co.uk

Conversational Branding

Piet Wulleman

When I first met you, you were cool
But it was game, you had me fooled
'cause 20 minutes after I gave you my number,
you already had my mailbox full

— "Bug A Boo," Destiny's Child

In 2006, we launched a campaign for IKEA. Among other things, the campaign featured a corporate blog. Looking back upon it, it was unidirectional, pushing an agenda and very uninviting to comment upon. It was part of a branding campaign, designed to build brand equity, and probably did nothing. Yet, since it was one of the fi rst corporate blogs in Belgium, it received a lot of att ention.

In 2009, we created two (clearly fictitious) Facebook characters for Samsung. We started topics, had people comment and start their own conversations. We went offline, interacted, and, although we knew in the end we wanted to communicate about the quality of the Samsung mobile phones, we were open to any turn the conversation could take. We didn't design for brand equity, but probably created it, and although we didn't cause a ripple on the surface, it built a loyal circle of members around … around what exactly? The Samsung brand? The characters? Not really sure — around the general idea, I guess.

What has changed between 2006 and 2009? We have started to embrace the defi nition of a brand as a shared idea, and have begun to let go of the idea of controlling a brand. And fi nally, we are learning every day to convince our clients to do just this.

Because that's what it comes down to — just do it.

This is supposed to be a practical book. A "time-to-get-serious" book. A how-to book. So how do you start? How did we get from IKEA to Samsung?

Here's an analogy. How do you stop smoking? By reading books? By convincing yourself how bad it is for health? By mentally preparing?

No. You just stop.

With branding-as-co-creation, it's the same thing. Just start doing it. Invite consumers to comment. Have them push your communication any direction they want. Let them redefine your brand. Take a deep breath, withstand the urge to intervene. Give hints and suggestions, but let people carry your brand.

Seducing people into your brand, then limiting the conversation to your terms and conditions, and bombarding them with the information you want to convey, is not a conversation. It's called "stalking."

You don't want to stalk. You don't want to be a bug a boo.

GERMAINE.be/glog

Branding Is Not About Your Ad Campaign

Efrain Mendicuti

Branding must be one of the most misused terms in marketing communications nowadays.

For fifteen years I've heard even some of the best marketers I've ever met say things like: "Let's do a branding campaign," "I need more branding in the ad" or "This sponsorship will give us great branding."

But branding is not something you just make up as you want.

Branding is, if nothing else, the most important and permanent thing we do about our brand.

Branding is an action. Everything we do is branding, yet branding is not simply about putting our logo on a banner or sponsoring an event or even about printing our brand image or concept onto something.

Branding is not about dressing up our delivery trucks with our brand image, yet the way our drivers drive and where and how they park says a lot about our brand.

A brand is a symbol that represents the core values of a company or a person. It is supposed to say and show what we are really all about.

"A brand is the idea and branding is the transmission of the idea," says Allen Adamson, author of *Brand Simple*.

Therefore everything we do exercises our brand, because each and everything we do and how we do it is a representation of our values, our principles, our ideas … our brand.

The way we do our advertising and marketing, how our organization supports causes and how each person in our organization conducts themselves day in and day out is branding.

So if we believe we can have better branding by changing our image or having a bigger logo, we need to think again.

We need to revisit the values and principles our brand represents and we need to think twice about ourselves, because no billboard, no website or TV ad is going to do better branding than how we behave ourselves.

THEDAILYANDTHENOTSO.BLOGSPOT.com

Is Your Brand Worthy of Attention?

Joe Pulizzi
ıııııııııııııııııııııııııı

If you are reading this book, you already understand that the way we used to market has come to an end. So long are the days where we could continually interrupt our customers and simultaneously increase sales.

The marketing profession itself has drastically changed. Fifteen years ago, we could count the number of marketing channels with our fingers. Today, there are limitless options available for communicating with customers, from websites to mobile apps to e-book readers.

Here's the rub. The more communication channels, the more customers work to ignore us. DVRs, satellite radio, spam filters, caller ID make it easy for customers to filter or deliberately ignore you. Your customers are fully trained in choosing what's worthy to engage in and what's not.

The answer to this challenge is actually quite easy, but hard for many to comprehend. Simply put, your brand needs to be worthy of attention. That's it. It's not calculus, it's simple math.

Not your products or services, but what you have to say. Your story. What you communicate on a consistent basis.

Is your brand worthy?

In the third *Indiana Jones* movie, the knight that guards the Holy Grail was chosen because he was the bravest, the strongest, and the most worthy of that honor. The same holds true for brands today. Customers will only engage with those brands that are the most helpful, most informative, most important to their lives and careers. Only the brands that are the most worthy are allowed into the customer conversation.

So what gets attention? Media does. Your favorite articles, books, songs, websites, online tools. Those things are worthy enough to get your valuable time.

To shape the conversation, to make an impact with customers, you need to develop media that is best of breed. Good enough is not good enough anymore.

So, what do you need to do now...?

1. Figure out how your brand will be different in one year. As your quest begins, how will customers see you as different, and how will that positively affect your business?
2. Your customer is the reader, the engager. What are the informational needs of your customers? You can and should be the solver of those pain points.
3. Set up listening posts. Your customers' wants and needs continually change. Where are you setting up listening posts to stay on top of what your customers needs are?
4. What channels and tactics will you leverage to prove your worthiness?
5. Who's the chief storyteller? Get someone to own the brand story to make sure you maintain *worthy* status.

Listen, hear, understand and answer (stir and continue). Be the helpful, trusted advisor. Be worthy of your customers' attention. Grow your business.

Brands Gain Nothing From Being Blowhards

David Weinfeld

I think we can all attest to having a friend or relative who has a tendency to dominate conversations. He likes to hear his voice so much so that you and everyone else can hardly get a word in edgewise. He drones on and on as if you weren't there. When you do finally get to say your piece, he never listens. He feigns attention so not to completely abuse your goodwill. His is the only opinion that matters.

Brands used to haphazardly treat people in the same manner that opinionated blowhards speak to their so-called friends. They thought they were engaging in conversation, but were really just listening to their own voices. Brands told their story as they saw fit, never stopping to ask consumers what they thought. They felt as though they never had to because consumers' voices were muted.

With consumers taking an active role in the conversation, ensuring that brands can no longer ignore them, two way dialogues are emerging which have the potential to elevate entire industries. The days of companies thinking they were always the smartest people in the room are over. They are beginning to see that there's nothing forcing consumers to listen to them tell the same stories *ad nauseam*. Just as the dominant voice in a false conversation loses its volume in an empty room, so too are brands left speechless when consumers ignore them to discover value elsewhere.

The strength of a conversation is derived from the value that both parties bring to it. When one side endeavors to take advantage of the other, playing on a perceived weakness, the conversation is over before it even starts. In the same way that push advertising is giving way to vibrant exchanges, brand conversations need to be as much about active listening as they are about speaking. To truly be heard, even if it's just by one person, is more powerful than a voice in an empty room could ever be.

Brands need to speak to consumers with honesty and trust. Rather than trying to manipulate conversations, advertisers need to embrace the power that consumers can give to their words. Even though giving up control of their brand messaging can be a scary proposition, companies need to forever realize that there's nothing to gain in being viewed as the opinionated blowhard. A conversation can't survive with only a single voice. A conversation thrives when voices are numerous and diverse thoughts are shared freely.

DSINSIGHTS.BLOGSPOT.com

And the Brand Played On

Steve Olenski

Welcome to my first foray into the *Age of Conversation*. Have a seat, take your shoes off … try the dip.

I've been asked to share some of my views on branding and how it relates to the wonderful world of online. You know… the place where the majority of your current and future customers reside.

So, about branding …

> *This brand is your brand, this brand is our brand … This brand was made for you and me.*

That of course was a paraphrase of the famous Woody Guthrie song, *This Land Is Your Land*. Funny, when you replace the word "land" with "brand" the meaning is still pretty much the same when used in this context.

Your brand is not yours. It's ours. All of ours. It just so happens right now we want to take your brand for a little joyride on the information superhighway. We're probably going to be on this ride for a while but rest assured, when we grow tired of this ride, another will come along to take its place.

But for now, if you are not engaging your customers online, someone else is. It's that simple.

Colonel Nathan R. Jessup: *"Are we clear?"*

Lt. Daniel Kaffee: *"Crystal."*

And before I forget, please do not mistake the word "engage" with the word "control."

> *Control is an illusion. You can't control the conversation, but you can control the effect … by staying in the conversation.*

So don't think for one second you go online, flash a brand … and make people nervous.

I clearly have watched entirely too many movies. But the paraphrasing of Colonel Jessup does have its merits. It doesn't matter if you're the biggest brand in the world or the smallest, you can't just set up shop online and expect people to flock to you, and control what they say and/or control what gets posted.

One of the many great things about taking your brand online is the immediacy with which you can receive feedback — albeit positive or negative. You know, you have to take the good with the bad and all that good stuff?

The key is to use what you glean from your customers, to listen to them, then act decisively and swiftly if need be because, guess what … they will be watching and waiting.

The bottom line — not including online strategy in your current marketing campaigns is like…working without an (inter)net.

THESTEVEOZONE.BLOGSPOT.com

Conversation as a Driver of Social Sustainability

Peter Korchnak

Social sustainability gets short shrift in branding. Reasons abound: it's hard to define and measure quantitatively; it's intangible, processual, and complex; it's not as sexy as caring for the environment and not as immediately profitable. No wonder the People bottom line stays in the background.

It doesn't have to be so. Define "brand" as the sum of your stakeholders' experiences with your company or product, and conversation as "the informal exchange of ideas by spoken word," then consider that conversation with the brand as part of the overall brand experience, and that the acquisition of ideas or information benefits both the brand and the stakeholder, injecting meaning into the interaction. Combine people, conversation, experience, and meaning, and social sustainability no longer appears so daunting.

Of course, people converse not with brands, but with other people. Every staff person interacting with a stakeholder engages in conversation on behalf of your brand, building the brand experience, creating meaning. Social media is one set of tools making brand conversations possible. Empowering your people with social media to converse with your stakeholders means shifting from centrally planned corporate messaging to decentralized, personal interactions that reflect the diversity of your staff.

People talk like people, not like press releases. If there's one principle to follow in conversing through social media for social sustainability, it's to emulate the way you'd talk in person. Converse online as you'd converse offline — no shouting, no one-way broadcasts, no corporate speak. As a company, set goals and measurable results and supply sufficient resources to follow through on your brand conversations. Then, let your people converse.

Like threads in a loom, the myriad of conversations your employees have with your stakeholders, through social media or other channels, will weave your brand into being. Thanks to consistent conversation, your brand will become more experiential, more conversational, and more human. What's more, by listening to, participating in, and engaging with your stakeholders' community, the conversation will enhance your social sustainability.

SEMIOSISCOMMUNICATIONS.com

Conversational Branding

Karalee Evans

In today's age of conversation, you may as well refer to it as the age of online conversation. Increasingly, brands are moving into the digital world, often with little foresight into what, why or how.

Simply being online doesn't mean you're having a conversation. The digital space has evolved and recognizes "tick-the-box" efforts of organizations. You need to be smarter and you need to know the rules of the channel before you venture into an earned space.

Many infl uential thought leaders from across marketing, public relations and digital media have contributed to discussions on what works best for a brand online. What doesn't seem to be featured, though, is a discussion on how to make a choice as to whether or not you should go online.

If you're the custodian of a brand where you've had success in establishing trust and credibility offline, you're in a prime position to move into the digital space, if it meets a need. Identifying what this need is, whether it's your own or your public's, is critical. It sets your objectives, it sets your direction and it sets your tone.

Social media rejects faceless, toneless, personality-less logos. Users demand personality, they demand interaction and (quite rightly) they demand authenticity. So, it's time to get busy and get a human voice.

Of course, conversation infers two-way interaction. So for public relations practitioners, marketers, brand managers, customer service teams and in fact, senior management of organizations, you need to be visibly listening to your customers and publics online.

You can invest in the software and human capital to listen online. There are a myriad of tools that effectively do this for you. But, the critical element of conversational branding online is to turn this listening into action. The action will be determined by what your product or service is, what your need is, what their need is, and what the conversation is asking for. Does a person on Twitter seem frustrated with your phone coverage? How can you, as a brand and a brand advocate, engage in a conversation that truly represents two-way communication?

The answer is simple. How would you start a conversation if your customers or publics engaged with you via a feedback form or made a complaint to your customer service staff?

Just because they're online doesn't mean you shouldn't engage. It actually makes it easier to hear their feedback and to target them for a conversation that will resonate.

JUSTANOTHERPRBLOG.WORDPRESS.com

60

The World Is Watching

Kevin Jessop

Everything you say and do has an impact on your brand. Read this again. **Everything you say or do has an impact on your brand.**

It's true that social media efficiently expands the audience to whom you communicate, but you need to apply caution to the conversation. Your words, pictures and other communications can be seen not only by friends, but also peers, customers and potential customers.

With an audience as diverse as that, you really need to pay attention to what you say.

I'm not a social media genius. I'm a guy with common sense. My approach to social media is this: don't *ever* commit to digital *anything* that could negatively affect your brand.

Posting a Facebook status that says "I want to smash my boss in the face" when he is on your friend list is an obvious no-no, but you'd be surprised by the more subtle, but equally devastating, conversational atrocities committed.

I once followed a guy on Twitter. He was a pretty influential and well-respected person in our community. He, a marketing manager for a well established company, always represented himself and his organization well to the Twitterverse — until he sent a direct message to his buddy, so he thought. By simply omitting a single character from his message, his private communiqué transformed into a very public memo detailing a rather niche adult movie he planned on watching that evening. The brand-crushing *faux pas* instigated complete abandonment of the company's social media strategy which ultimately resulted in a dramatic decrease in brand visibility.

My mum always says, "think before you speak" and she is so very right. As a brand, it's wise to steer away from politics, religion and extreme personal views (unless, of course, that is your goal). Being rude and arrogant is not a particularly good direction to take, either, and ridiculing and taunting other organizations or individuals is downright unprofessional.

Always keep your conversation in line with the brand values you wish to exhibit.

So, before you type your next status update in Facebook or Twitter remember **the world is watching**.

REFRESHINGRESEARCH.com

A Fork in the Road:
Enterprises at the Junction...

Peter Salvitti

"Do you see that road over there? Well, don't take that … it'll do you no good."

With that quotable of movie lines, Molouney, the train guard, gives Sean Thornton (John Wayne) a taste of what awaits him in Innisfree, Ireland, the bucolic setting of 1952's *The Quiet Man* (arguably John Ford's greatest movie triumph, though marred with some unflattering Irish stereotypes.)

What does this have to do with pitching social media? Nothing and everything; the setting of the movie is a tightly knit community that speaks with its own set of social *signals*. That communal *grapevine* is how things are said and done. Today's corporate enterprises are nothing like the community of Innisfree. Limitations and failings abound, the biggest of which is the lack of true inter-personal communication and collaboration, the *community*. Process rules the day but at the cost of dehumanizing the work force. Social media fundamentally is about the heightened *contextual* awareness needed to get things done.

An IT department is usually tasked with handling all technology in a project. This begins to limit the solution space necessary to solve the business problem. The conversation begins to shift from business-awareness to technology-*centricity*, inevitably leading to a myopic view of the business problem domain.

Ask any business stakeholder if there's a *particular* technology they'd like see used to solve a business problem, the answer will be "Huh, what?" Technology and tools are solution *enablers*, not the lens through which all solutions are modeled. A modern enterprise is beset with many contradictory mandates, but one thing is unvarying: the velocity of business keeps rising. Business functions in an enterprise must access information needed for various reasons (for example, enhanced customer service, speedier problem resolution, etc.) A methodology that promotes collaboration and cooperation is a top strategic goal. Any platform offering online social interaction holds promise, as it allows for more engaging and inclusive access to that information.

Forward-thinking enterprises needing to step up their responsiveness should pay attention to what social media offers — simpler communication, smarter information sharing and an inclusive approach to getting things done. Responding to shifting business opportunities demands that enterprises embrace social media; using social interaction architectures to harness the necessary contextual usage patterns is critical in getting closer to the customer and protecting the brand.

So? Do you see that social media road there? Well, it'll do you no good *if* you don't take it.

COLLABORATIVE.com/thought-leadership/white-papers

Measurement

Metrics Revolution

Craig Wilson

Anyone who says you can't measure social media impact either has rocks in their head or is simply ignorant of the benefits of a professional social media strategy.

Social media is entirely measurable once you have established your objectives. We do this at our agency every day. We know who we wish to reach, the message we wish to send and how to achieve and measure our business goals. In fact, 87 percent of our inquiries and 94 percent of our new business this year were generated via strategies dominated by social media. We strive to attain similar results for our clients.

Here's just one way it can work:

- Know the client you want to attract.
- Use a service like Google Keyword tools or nlyzr.com (in the interest of full disclosure, this is owned by my company) to discover the best keywords for your organisation to target.
- Post content on your company blog with a snappy title including these keywords. Your content should address solutions or issues in your industry rather than pure self-promotion.
- Optimize the post and website for the chosen keyword search.
- Provide easy ways for readers to find out more, to contact you or to leave their details.

Next:

- Use Tweetmeme to share the post on Twitter, and allow others to share it further.
- Use Digg, Delicious, Friendfeed, StumbleUpon, or Facebook to spread the word even further.
- Focus on the networks which work for you, especially the social media sites you use most.
- Repeat using slightly different keywords.

Now it is metrics time. Between the statistics provided by your chosen social networking and sharing tools, and your blog's statistics package or Google Analytics you will be able to reveal the effectiveness your campaign. Study these social media metrics carefully and regularly and you'll see ways to revolutionize your marketing.

You'll see how many times you've been re-tweeted, Dugg or Stumbled-Upon. You'll see the blog traffic, the traffic sources and the most effective keyword searches. You'll discover even better keyword searches to attack. Search rankings will reveal the effectiveness of your optimization. The number of leads and inquires generated will become obvious.

One site of ours has a post targeting a niche keyword search. Visitors from this search stay on the site for 20+ minutes, visit 6.7 pages and generate approximately six high-quality leads each week. This one post has delivered 47 percent of our new business this year.

That's the sort of measurement any marketer should love.

MEDIAHUNTER.com.au
GETSTICKY.com.au

The Social Media PAIDAY

Dennis Price

Just because something *can* be measured does not mean that it *should*.

The prevalence of digital marketing tools and technologies now lead marketers to measure everything that moves, paradoxically becoming paralyzed by the abundance of data points they previously yearned for.

Traditionally, marketers have embraced the AIDA funnel as a paradigm of customer engagement, moving the "prospect" through the various stages (awareness, interest, desire, and action) of increasing commitment. While this framework harks back to "old" marketing, the fundamentals are still profoundly relevant in the current marketing environment.

There is great depth of knowledge and increasing sophistication about appropriate metrics — from awareness through to the number of conversions, clicks etc. It is sensible and necessary to measure performance at each stage of the AIDA funnel.

But the problem with measuring isn't finding the appropriate metric. It is whether the metrics actually add up to something (the whole) which is more meaningful than the component parts.

The following acronym, PAIDAY, represents an extension of the traditional model for developing commercially meaningful customer engagement, and it provides a further crucial insight about measurement.

Purpose Attention Interest Desire Action Yield

The first letter in the funnel (P for purpose) is the overall aim (of your marketing activities) and the final letter (Y for yield) represents return on those activities.

The art of measurement science is picking a purpose that can and should be measured. Type and accuracy of measurement are merely distractions; relevance of measurement is the real issue.

The modern marketer's challenge is to understand, and then articulate, a purpose worth measuring, and then to define the metrics that that will govern the actions that will lead to the overarching purpose of your engagement.

There are many worthy objectives that cannot be measured, but in a commercial entity where you work with other people's money, striking the balance with demonstrable yield on an agreed purpose goes to the heart of the commercial enterprise. Marketing is not exempt, and social media will thrive if it can adopt a holistic view of all the metrics.

Don't measure things because you can. Measure what keeps you focused on your purpose. That is PAIDAY.

RETAILSMART.com.au

Measurable Should Not Be Used as a Synonym for Valuable

Jessica Hagy

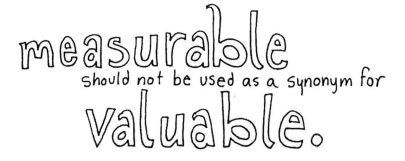

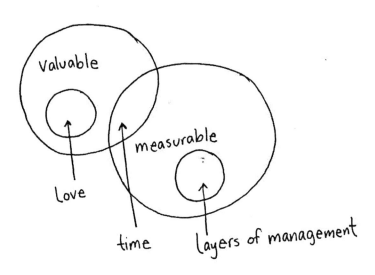

You are not your:

unique page views   carbon footprint

bank statements   market cap

twitter followers   box office returns

square feet of wall-to-wall carpet

direct reports   frequent flyer miles

Consumer ROI — Looking at Social Media Measurement from the Consumer's Perspective

Rick Liebling

It's conventional wisdom by now that social media has changed the dynamic between brand and consumer. Marketers speak of the paradigm shift that has taken place, putt ing more control — and influence — into the hands of the consumer. As a result, brands have embraced consumers like never before, engaging them online and making them part of the process.

Yet one thing hasn't changed despite the social media revolution. Companies still measure their marketing efforts based on a "brand-centric" approach. They look at things like Facebook friends or Twitter followers to determine *their* return on investment. But what if brands started to think about ROI in a manner that matched the emphasis they were putting on engaging consumers? What if rather than measuring *Brand ROI*, they measured *Consumer ROI*?

Every day consumers interact with brands in myriad ways, including commenting, sharing, creating, rating and reviewing. From blogging about a new product to watching the latest advert on YouTube, consumers are spending time (apart from money, *the* other consumer investment) with brands online. This is a fantastic development for the savvy marketer willing to invest in commitment marketing. But inevitably, consumers will soon be asking what they are getting for all this time and effort. As more brands look to engage consumers online, they (the consumers) will need to make decisions about which brands to spend their time with, and that decision will be made based on *Consumer ROI*.

Smart marketers will shift their measurement focus to a more "consumer-centric" approach, measuring the value consumers are receiving for their efforts and how the brands are bringing value to the consumer. How can brands measure *Consumer ROI*? From a quantitative standpoint, brands can measure the value they are bringing to consumers through brand-produced:

- Videos uploaded
- Blog posts
- Tweets
- Facebook content
- Online promotions/contests

But perhaps it's the qualitative metrics that are more interesting to think about. How is the brand acknowledging the consumers' investment? A brand that truly understands and appreciates a consumer's effort will:

- Link to a consumer's website
- Leave comments on a consumer's blog
- Re-tweet a consumer's comments
- Follow/friend a consumer

Consumer ROI will be a new concept for many brands, and the metrics are still being defined, but now is the time to take a different approach to social media measurement.

RICKLIEBLING.com

A Simple Conversation

Mark Hancock
ıııııııııııııııııııııııııııııııııı

[Sunday. 7.48pm. A father, son and golden retriever discuss social media measurement around a kitchen table somewhere in Wales.]

JH: Dad — what are you doing?

MH: I'm writing something for the AoC book like last year. I'm doing a bit on social media meaurement.

JH: How utterly fascinating!

MH: Sarcasm. Brilliant. You will make an excellent finance director when you grow up.

JH: What are you trying to measure anyway?

MH: The effects of people chatting and sharing stuff with their mates online, on mobiles and all that jazz.

JH: And what are the effects?

MH: People in marketing think the public will buy more stuff when they say and do nice things with a brand. They want people to buy more of their stuff so they're trying to make a case for spending money on getting people to have fun conversations around their product or services.

JH: How can you make people have more fun conversations?

MH: You can't. But you can be useful and interesting and hope people say nice things about your product — and then buy it and tell all their friends about it.

JH: How can you prove that someone saying nice things makes you or other people buy stuff?

MH: You can't. It might just build brand equity — those warm fuzzy feelings that make you feel good about something. But ultimately whatever your mate does influences what you do. If they like something, you're likely to like it, too — especially if it's something you can do together.

JH: Like PS3 I guess. But then I feel good about lots of things but don't want to buy them! We all liked the Burger King Facebook thing but none of us eat them. They're shit. And, I like Ferrari but can't afford one.

MH: You're making this tricky. And don't swear in front of the dog.

JH: Sorry. So, do you measure it like you measure all your other campaigns?

MH: Social media isn't a campaign — it's a program run over a long period of time and the proof that it works isn't trackable in the usual time periods. But you can track increased sales to people saying nice things over time if you set benchmarks and do it for long enough. Or you might find there is no correlation — so your screwed.

JH: So there is no real proof it works?

MH: Big companies use 90 day reporting to show shareholders a return on their investment so campaigns usually have to deliver a payback in that time. These programs can't do that in that timescale so most fail.

JH: But if it works, why not do it? Or, perhaps, they don't really work and you're all just kidding yourselves?

MH: No one can prove it works because they don't have measurements in place to track those effects over time. They also don't have money for it versus other campaign activity that does drive sales. And to make matters worse, the people selling these services are mostly not credible. Many have no real experience dealing with marketeers, which creates problems for others. Those campaigns that have measurable results have been purely sales focused and used specific digital channels. It has confused everyone, which is a pity.

JH: Sounds rubbish. Also sounds like you can't really prove it either.

MH: Correct. Go get Daddy another beer.

ıı

HOLYCOWTHINKS.com

The Quantitative Conundrum

Doug Mitchell

When I speak to groups about social marketing, question one is, "How do I measure success?" I respond, "How about more sales?" This "truthiness" is apparently not common among the new media crowd because I typically elicit crooked faces. Of course we desire increased customer satisfaction, lower cost marketing, and increased audience engagement. But where the rubber meets the road … is sales revenue.

Tracking and attributing increased revenues to the strategic use of social marketing is challenging. But is it any more challenging than tracking results from an ad in a magazine, phone book, or trade journal? Does your firm walk around with ROI numbers handy from that $2500/month phone book ad? Probably not. I suggest that the following methods be deployed to ultimately tie social marketing efforts to sales results.

- **Use hyper-targeted micro-niche content to drive a conversion.** A conversion may be an actual sale of a widget online. It could be a sign up for an email marketing campaign. If you are doing keyword and market research, you can hone in on very specific groups and craft a message specifically for them. You can track this campaign with internal analytics, CRM, or other systems to plot the initial contact to close-of-sale pathway. Too many marketing efforts are "throw it against the wall and see what sticks." Today's consumer whether digital native or retired boomer increasingly demands targeted marketing efforts.

- **Accept that social and interactive marketing efforts are your marketing efforts.** This seems obvious but business in America is dodging this reality. We don't walk around expecting that 100 percent of our marketing department is always doing something with a direct ROI. They are often tasked with creating things that don't "auto-convert" into a sale. Same goes with social and interactive marketing efforts. However, strategic participation in online communities, chat, Twitter, Facebook et al can yield metrics that can be tied to sales. "We have built 1500 followers online and get an average of 14 clicks per tweet when we put out information and 34 clicks when we put out an offer." If you're keeping good client data, you'll know how many closed sale clients are following you and participating in your online communities.

Is this an exact science? No. But when's the last time you put metrics to the telephone and email? Don't, or you might toss them both.

CREATEWOWMEDIA.com

Beyond Measurement

Mark Avnet

"Not everything that counts can be counted, and not everything that can be counted counts." Relativity *and* common sense — Einstein rocked.

It doesn't take an Einstein to know that we spend a lot of time, energy and money counting things, many of which don't really help us — we count them because we've always counted them, or simply because they're countable.

Our job is to think about what drives behavior and attitudes, how we can be influential in ways that help people accomplish their goals and also support the needs of our clients. And then to look at ways that mediating technologies can be used to facilitate those goals.

Although quant methodologies can provide useful information, they often miss out on the human element — we have to intuit what those numbers mean. And they're too easy to attach to the wrong driver — for example, are people using a site's search function because they want to explore the richness of a site, or because the site isn't designed well and they're lost?

Instead of guessing, let's ask them.

There are many ways to ask about the "why" of behavior. Our industry uses focus groups a lot, in spite of research that shows they often can't be relied on.

There are other kinds of tests coming out of psychological and communication sciences — things like "implicit association tests," which can be used to identify things that are associated in people's minds by thin-slicing responses. I use hypnosis as an adjunct to more traditional psychological methods to quickly find out what's happening in the subconscious mind. Gerald Zaltman's patented techniques use imagery to create consensus maps. Clotaire Rapaille mines what he calls the "reptilian brain" to uncover the subconscious drivers of behavior.

What these techniques have in common is the goal of understanding the emotional forces behind what we do, what Dan Hill calls "Emotionomics." This is important because emotions trump intellect as an actionable force, no matter how evolved we think we are. We primarily use intellect to justify a decision we've already made emotionally.

It takes descriptive language to capture, store and communicate these emotions.

We need to remember that our branded and unbranded communications are between people, and people are not binary, on/off, quantifiable sorts of creatures.

We need to move towards understanding context, emotions, needs, the unconscious but powerful motivators, if we're to be good communicators.

Even if these things are harder to "count" — they matter.

BRANDCENTER.VCU.edu
CONVERGINGARTS.com

How Long Is This Piece of String? (Unveiling the World's First Use of 3-D Measures in Print)

David Petherick

Da 1st Measure: Definition

You'll never find *any* success if you don't start out by *defining* success.

So first, set out what you want to achieve: +36.5 percent direct sales? +114 percent web visitors on afternoons? Recognition from the boss? Top 10 ranking for five keyword phrases in Yahoo & Google? -62 percent spend on radio ads while maintaining new visitor traffic? Replace mailshots with email, RSS or Twitter for a significant number of customers?

If you don't know what you are aiming for, quite aside from missing, you will find it very difficult to measure the things that got you there! So sit down and answer the simple question — *what do I want to achieve here* — and thus, what resources should I commit?

Da 2nd Measure: Devices

Five measuring tools:

1. **Getclicky.com** — excellent '2.0' analytics tool to measure web traffic, actions on site and sources. Free and paid options.
2. **Google Analytics** —self-explanatory web traffic measurement tool. Free. See www.google.com/analytics
3. **Google Webmaster Tools** — essential to make sure your site is indexed by Google correctly. Free. See www.google.com/webmasters
4. **CoTweet.com** — superb tool to allow teams to collaborate on a single, or multiple Twitter accounts. Free and paid options.
5. **Trackur.com** — tracks mentions of your products, people or brands across social media, so you can easily respond to otherwise "unknown" issues and individuals. Paid, with free trial.

There is a fuller description of each tool at http://bit.ly/aocaoc*

Da 3rd Measure: Dumbness

> *"Not everything that can be counted counts, and not everything that counts can be counted."*
> — Albert Einstein

Not counting counts for little when dealing with your online reputation — so use tools to listen, monitor and help you understand what people say about you, and to join the conversation. Silence can only be appropriate when you are not, by your absence, oblivious.

You can't be everywhere, you can't always be perfect, but if you *define* what you are trying to achieve, and *measure* how you're performing, you're already doing better than the other guys — and will delight customers, stakeholders, and yourself. In 3-D!

DIGITALBIOGRAPHER.com

*Disclosure: Getclicky and Trackur will pay me if you pay to use their tools via my links. I will, of course, measure this!

Your Brand Is a Series of Bad Dates, But Who's Really Counting?

Andy Hunter

Is your brand a bad date in the social marketing scene? I'm guessing if you've been thoughtful enough about social marketing to read this you can't be all that bad. But then again, I bet you don't quite have them lining up at your digital doorstep either. How can you tell if you're brand is a bad date? Keep track of how you are doing? Let's see how you measure up:

You watch what they are doing and take a lot of notes (traditional measures semantic analysis). You've read all the experts I see. Social media is about listening, observing what you hear. You're counting how many times your fans and detractors have good (and bad) things to say about you. Now, nobody's going to ding you for listening, but let's be sure to do something with all those measures and scores. Otherwise, well … you're closer to a stalker than a good date.

You send a lot of messages and from what you can tell they're getting read (volume-click metrics). Clicks, opens, mentions, follows, link-throughs etc. You send out messages and people seem to be reading them. But what do you have to say next? What are people doing with those litt le conversational gestures? Remember, people aren't looking for quantity and counts when interested in stimulating conversations and people. Whether it's the first contact or 10-year anniversary, keeping things interesting makes a difference.

Things are great, but you (or your date) is invisible to friends (participation and advocacy). You might be great, but all that one-to-one time is going to get pretty boring after awhile. So question, what are you doing to have more fun with your friends and brand neighbors? Everyone knows a good party gets people talking, sharing and having a good time. Throw a brand party now and then and keep tabs on how much fun your guests are have before and after the bash.

So what the heck does this mean to marketing and social media measurement? It's pretty simple, really. Transactional measures don't test the strength of relationships. Sentiment and scores don't uncover what people think, do and say with the things you share. Ask yourself how your own *reciprocal measures* add up first, then see how they're responding with *brand love, brand advocacy and brand participation* of their own.

EXPERIENCEFREAK.com

Social Media ROI — Stop Worrying and Get to Work!

Ian Lurie

"But we can't measure the ROI."

That's the excuse I've heard time and again. It's how nervous managers shut down exploration of social media. My only answer: Get off your arse and try it. Here's why —most ROI is intangible.

Did you consider ROI before you decided to be courteous to customers? Did you calculate ROI before organizing your store? Ponder the ROI of answering the phone? Or having a clean, orderly waiting area in your office?

You did it because you *just knew it made sense*. The ROI is intangible. You know you'll get a return from all of those activities. They cost money and time. But you do them anyway.

Social media is another intangible generator of ROI. Helping a potential customer on Twitter is like a sincere greeting when they enter your store: It establishes a connection that increases the chances of a sale. You don't justify good customer relations with ROI. Social media establishes those relationships. If you want good customers and a successful business, you'll stop reading here and go get to work.

Blurry Boundaries

You can't easily determine where social media starts and stops. The work you do with social media supports:

- Search engine optimization
- Offline marketing
- Customer outreach and loyalty/rewards programs
- Brand awareness.

Every positive experience a customer has with you makes their next interaction more likely to succeed. Social media provides that experience.

OK, fine. Maybe you need a little more encouragement. Here's what you can measure.

What You Can Measure — ROE

Maybe you can't measure return on investment. But you can measure the return on engagement. Learn to use tools like Tweetmeme Analytics, Bit.ly's click tracking, Google Alerts and Feedburner's RSS feed tracking. Start recording clicks, re-tweets, mentions and tweets. Also, keep score. Each time someone in your organization interacts with a potential customer via social media, record it. Track all of these numbers over time. Track sales at the same time. Do it for six months. Notice anything?

- Do sales go up?
- Are you getting sales from previously unknown segments of your audience?
- Are sales steady in spite of a bad economy?
- Are you getting more repeat customers?

Stop thinking about return on investment. Start thinking about return on engagement.

Stop making excuses, and get to work!

CONVERSATIONMARKETING.com

Measurement

Anjali Ramachandran

The question I usually ask anyone who broaches the subject of measuring social media is how they'd measure conversations at a party. You get a group of people together, and hope they (and you) will have a good time. Some may and some may not, and all of it is not really within your control, even if you do your best to ensure that the canapés, drinks and music are all perfect. It's about people, ultimately, and people can't exactly be controlled.

You can't control interactions online beyond a point either. When brands engage in conversations with their audience in the digital sphere, they do so in the *hope* that these interactions will lead to increased monetary returns for the brand, and/or an improved brand image. Some people may be of the opinion that measuring their investment in social media isn't for them — take care of the small things, as Emily Dickinson said, and the big things will take care of themselves. That's a very enlightened view to take, but not one that is often espoused. As a marketing manager, it is only natural to want to understand the returns of your investment.

The first thing that will help in answering the "how do you we measure social media" question is answering the "what am I looking to measure" question first. Is it having a certain number of comments on a blog post? Getting people to contribute ideas to a wiki? Making sure they spend x amount of time on a site? Perhaps it is maximizing the number of mentions of your brand on the digital sphere, or solving a certain number of customer issues via Twitter. Whatever it is, one person's definition of success is likely to differ from another's, and articulating your metrics for success at the beginning will enable measuring it to your satisfaction better than otherwise.

The discussion on measuring social media has now rightfully evolved into a discussion on measuring engagement, as initiatives such as the Altimeter Group's *EngagementDB* report (for brand engagement) indicate (see www.engagementdb.com). Even more important however, is measuring consumer engagement, through simple metrics like the number of comments on a post or forum. Engaged and regularly returning visitors to a site can be converted into superusers if they are sufficiently rewarded, who in turn are the foundation for a solid community. And communities are the foundation of a society.

ANJALIR.WORDPRESS.com

The Best Metric — Positive Mentions

Douglas Hanna

Companies that are just starting to explore Twitter and the blogosphere often get overwhelmed by the pure quantity of conversations and discussions happening at any given time. Big name brands are discussed thousands of times a day by just as many different people and this can be overwhelming to anyone charged with quantifying any sort of social media presence.

A method that many companies have embraced and have used to track their relative success and popularity within the social media sphere is positive mentions of the company's name or a phrase that is important to the company (for example, a product name).

Tracking positive mentions is a worthwhile endeavor for a few reasons:

1. Positive mentions are easy to identify and can be easily picked out among a group of mentions
2. Keeping tabs on positive mentions allows the company to see who is advocating for the company and its products and services. This information can be useful for customer service and loyalty tracking, marketing and more
3. Positive mentions can be used as testimonials and to help generate additional business. They can also be used to motivate customer support staff and help boost morale.

Keeping a record of both the number of mentions and the content of the mentions is essential. Just having a count of positive mentions is not nearly as useful as having the content of the mentions as well. Customer feedback is fundamentally qualitative and loses a lot of its value if it is reduced to purely quantitative terms.

Companies can also track negative mentions of their brand around Twitter and the blogosphere. Though different in philosophy, both approaches are equally effective and work towards accomplishing essentially the same goal — gaining a quantitative understanding of the company's social media presence.

When it comes time to identify the relative success of a presence on social media sites, having accurate, quantitative data is essential. A general idea is useful, but it will be hard to convince the higher ups that a social media campaign is working without any sort of data.

SERVICEUNTITLED.com

Begin Measurement with the Business Outcome in Mind

Adelino de Almeida

The first question that comes to mind when faced with the seemingly chaotic environment of social media — is whether we can measure it at all. The answer is that we can … but we need to shift our frame of mind from the idea that it can be measured like direct mail, or that it can be inferred like mass media measurements. Social media is its own animal that requires a new set of metrics and a new approach.

To that end, we need to bear in mind that social media measurement focuses on measuring connections and the transmission of messages, not on the measurement or evaluation of the people at each end of the connection. Social media measurement breaks cleanly from the need to know in detail what each participant in a conversation looks like, it focuses instead on what is being said and how often it is said. The closest we ever get to knowing something about those involved in the conversation is when we need to quantify their level of influence.

Measuring social media is straight forward but requires considerable mathematical knowledge.

To establish a solid measurement methodology, refer to that used for media mix modeling:

- Begin by defining the business outcome metric — sales, brand awareness, preference, etc. There is a smaller subset for social media than for mass media measurement
- Identify the data sources and collect data — identify all the relevant sources that can be tapped: blogs, product reviews, tweeter feeds, social networks, etc. The trick here is to track communications that are relevant, and for that we need to evaluate the influence or authority of those that participate in the conversation, see below for details

A suggested list of metrics entails:

- Frequency of positive and negative references — distinguish between general comments about the brand from those that are specific to a given product or offer
- Average weight or authority of the person that originates the message — this is a good area to use Social Network Analysis methods
- Momentum — how far does the message propagate in the network before it dies off
- Persistence — how long does the message or meme persist.

Finally, employ a method that establishes causation between the metrics and the business outcome — explore the use of time series if the data is rich enough or that of structural equation modeling if it isn't.

ADELINO.TYPEPAD.com

Social Marketing and Measurement

Peter Komendowski

ⅢⅢⅢⅢⅢⅢⅢⅢⅢⅢⅢⅢⅢⅢⅢⅢⅢⅢⅢⅢⅢⅢⅢⅢ

Excerpts from *The Discussion on Economic Gravity.*

The success of marketing is measured by the influence of marketing on elements that have measurable components — for example, money as an indicator of economic benefit. In a world of advertising where big has often been presented as better, social marketing has been forced to conform to performance criteria not always appropriate for measurement on a socially significant level. This demands that we question whether traditional media measurement tools are suited to the effective evaluation of social marketing.

Just as the bottom line is readily accepted as a measure of business performance, the influence of marketing, and the ability to measure the influence of marketing, is pervasive because of its ability to identify and examine indicators, accumulate data sets, establish relevant performance criteria, and ultimately test the results. Realtime physical comparisons (or measurement) simply mean verifiable quantitative data — in the vernacular of sales, "comparing apples to apples." Ad agencies and media outlets are notorious for reaching radically different conclusions about similar markets, a trend that has done little to build confidence in media measurement.

Herein lies a conundrum — "marketing is viewed as an expense rather than an expression of a healthy business model."

In the recent past, little effort was expended to explore the relevant relationships between products and the market connectors that are the domain of advertising and marketing value decisions. Few firms have in place a method for measuring marketing performance that inspires confidence in the expense. This is most evident when it is noted that the first budgets to be cut in tough times are those for marketing and media.

It is certainly no surprise that "social media" ride a wave of relatively inexpensive technological advances as the darlings of business markets interested in saving money by redefining reach and frequency in the context of staggering, even if somewhat ephemeral, numbers. Numbers, which by comparison to traditional marketing vehicles can make little bottom line sense. Like the proverbially human test of belief in gravity (jumping off the roof of a barn and trying to fly for example), a financial statement (like the ground) serves as a reminder of the obvious truth.

For all of the proliferation of new media and social marketing, have we done more than shuffle the deck with mixed results in favor of the theory that new is better?

If social marketing is going to become viable and avoid the historical pitfalls of traditional marketing, we are going to have to put the word "measurement" back into the vernacular of good business and define it in such a way that works for all forms of marketing.

Marketing is vested in idea that the core values of a business are intrinsic to its connections to a market. The ability to understand and measure market forces is as essential to a healthy business as gravity is to a healthy earth. It is an organic relationship, identifiable and measureable, of which we understand the benefits and limitations.

The challenge of measuring the effectiveness of marketing is a priority for today's media managers. While social marketing has done a great deal to promote the benefits of new media, it has raised serious issues about measurement. If social marketing is going to unlock new opportunities, marketers will have to build measurement tools that work across the broad range of marketing opportunities and rebuild confidence in marketing as an essential and vital aspect of a successful business.

ⅢⅢⅢⅢⅢⅢⅢⅢⅢⅢⅢⅢⅢⅢⅢⅢⅢⅢⅢⅢⅢⅢⅢⅢⅢⅢ

BOTTOMLINEZEN.com

Global Measurement for ~~Global~~ All Businesses

Michelle Chmielewski

Certain social media measurement tools have made great advancements in automatically determining human sentiment behind a statement. They can filter information about your company and products/ services so that you not only know *how much* people are talking about your brand, but how they *feel* about it.

However, the majority of these tools are only designed for the English language.

"Good enough," you might say. But what's stopping you from becoming an international company?

Measuring social media interactions in multiple languages can help you

1. **Analyze threats and opportunities.** Stay on top of current events that will affect your industry, and create or discover windows of opportunity. Expanding abroad is always a risky move, but you can offset that risk by conducting preliminary international market research with the click of a mouse, and discover more about foreign environments before making costly decisions.

2. **Leverage your strengths and mitigate your weaknesses.** You have no control over the socioeconomic environment, and may or may not have any influence over the legislative, political, and technological environments. You do have control over how you react to it. Exploit your business's strengths by finding out what consumers in other countries find helpful about your products or your competitors', or what they wish could be better.

3. **Know your customers to increase your revenues.** You can listen to consumers on the free instant-messaging service QQ in China, Orkut in Brazil and India and Hi5 in many parts of Central and South America, or any number of international consumers on Twitter — even with free monitoring tools. With so many options available to find new customers, what's stopping you? By monitoring in foreign languages, not only can you find them, you can find out what is the acceptable Internet etiquette for approaching them without coming off as a spammer.

4. **Cut communication and marketing costs.** Connect with local resources and professionals that are familiar with your industry in their country. They can be your intermediators, along with influential bloggers that already have the ears of your potential customers. A 2009 Nielsen survey showed that people are most likely to trust the advice of people they know and trust the opinion of consumers who post comments online. If your customers are listening, you should be, too, to reduce direct marketing costs, product development costs, customer service costs — the possibilities are endless.

5. **Make more money.** Increased revenue + decreased costs = increased profit. So no matter what the language:

$$$

SYNTHESIO.com

The DANGER of Measurement

Phil Osborne

The human desire to understand (and ultimately control) things has been responsible for many great discoveries and advances. However there is a dark side to the world of "metrification," especially for the social media field. The clue is in the bracketed phrase above — the control aspect.

Taking an organizational perspective on any phenomena, it is not long before the "How do we manage it?" question is posed. This is entirely appropriate in the organizational paradigm in which the efficient and effective allocation of resources can lead to competitive advantage. It's also easy to agree with (particularly in the desired sustainable future) because who would want to deliberate waste things by being inefficient? And you can't manage what you don't measure!

So a measurement chapter is required in any social media book, to get credibility in the boardroom and prove the "value" of the Facebook/ YouTube/ Twitter campaign, right?

As undoubtedly demonstrated by other contributors in this book, you can measure social media. In fact, in researching my contribution I reconsidered what I was going to submit based on excellent insights and logical substantiation provided by luminaries such as Beth Kanter and Jim Sterne (see http://bit. ly/7qq6mF). However, the existence of metrics does not change the basis of my concern. If the purpose of measuring is ultimately control, then there is a significant consequence that must be considered before adopting any metric (or measurement program).

Marketing has experienced this consequence before. Who hasn't heard of "customer relationship management" (the ubiquitous CRM), designed to enhance relationships, engender loyalty and increase both purchase frequency and propensity! The fantastic funnel filler, supported by comprehensive metrics, industry benchmarks and best practice advice. How is that going for you, the customer, on the end of this managed relationship? In my experience, both as manager and the managed, not many of us like managed relationships (and don't stay in them for long).

So, now we are seeking to manage conversations and social interaction? The fate of this has been revealed already (*Cluetrain Manifesto* anyone?). Be afraid, because I for one worry that metricification, as currently practiced, has a limited place in a post industrial economy in which the hegemony of production is being supplanted by collaboration, co-creation and customer centricity.

Social media can easily go the same way as CRM. Be careful what you wish for.

OTAGO.ac.nz

Measure Social Media ROI the Dell Way

Jeff Larche

Conversations have always led to brand discovery. Someone talks about how a product solved a problem. Someone replies with an even more compelling review of a different product. More people interject. By the time the topic shifts, one or more product trials have been triggered. It's a brand manager's nirvana, but one that has — until now — been abjectly unquantifiable.

It used to be that the best a brand manager could hope for, with her limited arsenal of broadcast and print ads, was hearing the stories that would burble up from the sales floor. For example, she might know her campaign is working when consumers walk up to salespeople with, "My coworkers and I saw your ad last night and got to talking."

Technology has changed everything. First, the corporate web site is now a proxy for the sales floor. Before consumers talk to a salesperson they can arrive at a site and kick the tires virtually. The other big change is the advent of *digital* conversations — or, more importantly, the advent of measuring traffic from those conversations, whether they're from Twitter, Facebook, Yelp — wherever.

Meet the new sales-tracking source codes. Now you don't need anecdotal reports from salespeople. These codes can report, in great detail, how many of your sales came from folks who "heard it through the grapevine."

Source codes aren't perfect. They usually measure traffic in a single web session, starting with arrival from a blog or microblog link and leading through to the final inquiry form or purchase confirmation. On the other hand, source codes can sometimes report all you need to know.

Just ask Dell. They announced in June of 2009 that they had hit $3 million in sales to people clicking through from Twitter posts.

My advice to those seeking to measure social media impact: Start with the obvious. Measure the most trackable sales and inquiries by setting up source codes — one for each social media site that can generate a click to your site. Then have your deputized bloggers and "Tweeters" use these codes in their embedded URLs.

If you're using Google Analytics, your analytics manager can find help on my blog. It's a step-by-step tutorial for setting up the codes in Google. Just go to DigitalSolid.com and type "snurl" into the search box.

Then start measuring conversations "the Dell way," and let me know your own success story.

DIGITALSOLID.com

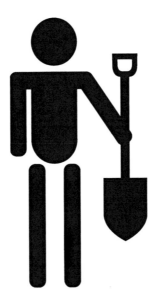

Corporate Conversations

Building the Social Enterprise

Toby Bloomberg

Once upon a time there was a CEO who worked diligently for many years building a successful company. One day she (or perhaps it was he) realized the business model she had carefully crafted was no longer valid. She found that her customers and prospects were not waiting for her website to be updated, new ads to launch, sales calls returned or direct mail pieces received in order to make purchase decisions. She discovered that customers were not in company service queues for answers to their questions.

Something called the "social web" had created a world where people exchanged ideas, information and opinions as easily as if they were chatting over a cup of coffee at their favorite café. In exploring these conversations she was surprised to learn many were not only about her company's brands but its service, employees and the enterprise itself. "Could this information be valuable research to learn about our customers?" she thought.

Our CEO was one smart lady. She did not want to replace traditional strategy with a shiny new toy. However, the idea of customers engaging in the digital world about her brands intrigued her; she set out to understand how social media impacts not only customers, prospects and stakeholders but employees and current business processes.

She convened a cross functional task force that included people from digital, marketing, consumer insights, HR, customer care, IT, operations, PR, legal, sales and accounting. Creating an environment where people could safely discuss their concerns she encouraged them to look at challenges/fears and opportunities that social media brings to the enterprise.

Team members then were charged with researching and reporting about social media through the lens of: competition, industry trends, customer participation and expectation and company culture. In addition, each team member was asked to actively experience at least one new media tool.

With the company's business objectives in clear sight, subsequent sessions focused on the impact of social media to each department, as well as, the company culture. It became obvious new processes would have to be developed and integrated throughout the enterprise: cross functional communication systems, hiring qualifications changed include the ability to work in a team environment and *customer focused* would have to be redefined across all channels.

The CEO sighed. Becoming a Social Enterprise wouldn't happen over night but building a stronger organization with better brands always took time.

There is plenty of coverage of social media when the focus is on marketing or advertising. But what is happening in other parts of your business? How is social media playing within your business and has it surprised you? Or ... if you're a consultant or agency, how do you introduce social media to the C-level at your client's business? How do you make social media more than a fad or seem relevant to the bottom line?

DIVAMARKETINGBLOG.com

Corporate Conversations

Eric Brody

We regularly interface with our clients' Boards and senior leadership given that our work involves creating and revitalizing brands. Across organizations, our conversations have always taken on similar themes. However, over the past couple of years, amidst discussions of visions, missions, goals and strategies, the topic of social media has also found its way into our conversations.

At this point in the social media lifecycle, we're not really *introducing* the concept to clients. There's enough conversation going on, enough statistics, war stories and success stories, that it's top of mind for any market-led senior executive.

Leadership is, at least, vaguely aware that social media can help build transparency and help reclaim consumer trust. They know the conversations that are independently taking place around them can impact their company's reputation and bottom line. And they know (rationally) that they can't hide under a rock. But leadership tends to be confused and nervous about how to begin to respond and get engaged.

There's no right way to tactically address these issues. But there are right starting points:

First, social media shouldn't drive the conversation. As important as it is to future success, both image and impact wise, it is still a tactic. It must be framed in goals and strategies, the social media practices of your customers, and a business case.

Second, you can't ignore social media. To do so is like fighting gravity. While the tools will change, the conversations are not going to go away. At a minimum, you must start to listen. Leadership can gain valuable insight into the "hot buttons" of their industries and customers. In turn, you can tap new audiences and potential new revenue streams.

Third, while striving for perfection is admirable, it's a waste of time when it comes to social media. Because unlike developing an ad where you test, tweak and get your message just right, truly open dialogue is impossible to control. With social media, you're always going to be learning, growing and adjusting. You need to follow the lead of your customers. They'll let you know what content is relevant, and how best to engage them.

Fourth, consider social media alongside, and not a replacement for, traditional media. There will always be a need to generate eyeballs. Use the reach of traditional to help you find and then engage audiences in more meaningful, personal, trusted and two-way social media conversations.

ERICBRODYSBLOG.com

Presenting a Business Case for Social Media to the Corner Office

Beth Wampler

In the corporate world, all decision-making comes down to the bottom line. Mr. or Ms. CEO has to decide "Will this make money, save money or protect me from losing money?"

So how do you convince the CEO that social media is good for the bottom line? It can be hard to monetize. Just what is it worth to have 5000 Facebook fans? Or to be followed by 2500 Twitterers? What's the ROI on enabling your customers to talk back?

To make a business case for social media, first go back to marketing basics. Social media is simply a new channel of communication, like radio, direct mail or events. It's too big to ignore or treat as a fad. It needs to be figured into your strategic mix as one element of an integrated marketing effort. Second, every marketer knows that each medium has advantages for reaching certain audiences. You wouldn't use the *Wall Street Journal* to reach tweens, right? Same with social media. It's not right in every situation or for every message. But social media can be a powerful tool to gain relevancy with certain market segments, including IT audiences, teens and twenty-somethings, even moms. If social media is part of your prospect's life, it needs to be part of your marketing mix.

Here's a real-world example. Financial institutions are having a hard time attracting customers in the 18–34 demographic. This demographic doesn't read newspapers anymore, broadcast is so fractured that reach is hard and expensive to accomplish, and to top it off, this audience is extremely skeptical of marketing. Some smart banks and credit unions are using social media as part in their outreach strategy to this market. One credit union in Colorado, for example, created a blog where members can share their stories about interactions they've had with the credit union. Some of those stories then become source material for ad campaigns aimed at drawing in younger members. From getting their first car loan, to learning what a credit score is and why it's important, members have shared stories that are not only relevant to this audience, but also break the skepticism barrier and ring true. Because they are!

Engaging customers in this way — bringing them into the conversation — is invaluable. And with little or no hard costs required — only someone's time — social media can make a lot of bottom line sense.

THINKAOR.com

Adding Social Sizzle to Internal Communications

Amy Mengel

So much social media excitement is focused on how brands engage with consumers that we often forget that these new Web technologies are great for internal communication, too. Engaged employees can often make the best brand ambassadors. Here are a few ways to incorporate social media into an internal corporate communications program.

Video

How many employees actually read those 1500 word missives the CEO sends each week (even if they're craftily ghost written by a communicator)? Maybe a handful. Record the message with a web cam instead. Execs will love it because it takes less time than the back-and-forth editing of a written piece, and employees will connect more with a live person than stiffly-written corporate updates. Embed the video on the company intranet and allow employees to rate or comment on it.

Wikis

Version control on a document has been the downfall of many a project. With dozens of people working across time zones, emailing around a document for review can result in a mishmash of input. Set up an internal wiki for a project that allows team members to edit, review, comment and approve aspects of a project so that everyone's on the same page.

Internal Networks

Use the web to exploit the "weak ties" among employees. A product developer in India may be struggling with a problem that a technologist in Brazil has expertise in. Create an employee skills database that's internally searchable and allows them to fill out a profile with their interests, expertise and qualifications and post requests. Don't have the resources to build out your own system? Try creating a private LinkedIn Group for your employees (just make sure they're not sharing company-sensitive information).

Gather Feedback

If you're thinking of implementing a new system or policy, pilot it at a single location first, but allow the employees there to publicly express their thoughts about it via an internal microsite. Most importantly, *listen*. Take their feedback to heart and make changes to the program before it's rolled out company-wide.

Develop Knowledge Communities

Create forums for a particular function, process, or project and allow employees to ask and answer questions. Incentivize them for participating — not necessarily with money — it can be as simple as giving them points or a ranking based on their answers (think Yahoo! Answers). Make it easy for employees to draw on their coworkers' knowledge and show off their own.

AMYMENGEL.com

Facebook Fundraising

Katie Smith McIntyre

It's clear that social media is not a fad—it's definitely here to stay. What's uncertain is how these applications will evolve. What began as different ways for friends to connect online has progressed into marketing tools most businesses are remiss in ignoring. In fact, touting oneself as a social media expert is becoming big business in itself as companies scramble to understand this trend and how to use it to their advantage. I've attended numerous webinars recently with tips on pitching social media to executive leadership as a necessity, not just a time waster on the company dime.

At my day job, I'm still attempting to fully immerse my organization in a social media strategy. While the tools are free, it does require extra staff hours at a time when many workloads are already stretched to the limit. My co-workers and I often joke that some companies must be hiring interns to make bi-hourly posts. Who really has time to do this? Doesn't one eventually run out of things to say? After all, posting "I'm eating a sandwich" doesn't do much for the bottom line.

Despit this hurdle, I recently found great success for a minimal time commitment using social media, specifically Facebook, for fundraising. I organized a group of *Run to Remember* participants for the IMT Des Moines Marathon. *Run to Remember* is a race training and fundraising initiative for the National Hospice Foundation. As part of the program, participants create personal fundraising pages via active.com for friends and family to verbally and financially support their efforts.

This year participants also promoted the race on Facebook and were pleasantly surprised when friends they hadn't spoken to in years suddenly became supporters. Through status updates, they were able to post information about the race and their training progress without feeling intrusive. It was also a great way to provide gentle reminders to those who said they'd contribute but had forgotten. The key for these participants was mixing some of the fun, personal updates (like the aforementioned sandwich reference) with those promoting the race.

The use of social media to raise funds and friends for this race was definitely a success. We look forward to repeating our experience for future races as well as incorporationg new tools as they transpire.

More information about *Run to Remember* may be found at www.runtoremember.com.

KDSVOICE.WORDPRESS.com

Implement a Vision, Not a Tool

Stefan Erschwendner

Social media has gotten a lot of hype over the last years, especially in the field of marketing and communication. It seems that every brand feels the need to be on Facebook and on Twitter to spread messages and enter the conversation. Many companies seem to put collaboration, sharing and social media on the same level. But there is an important difference.

Social media alone is not the solution. It is a tool like email or SAP. People will change behavior and adopt tools for a vision that influences corporate culture, not because of a tool. It is the vision that makes the difference and gives people a reason to act. Every vision needs its tools and social media is a powerful one. A tool, however, is not a game changer whereas providing vision and a sense of direction can be.

Many organizations fail to create cultures of collaboration, knowledge sharing and conversation that go beyond cultures of silos. It's not surprising that many corporations are struggling thanks to narrow thinking and limiting structures. Innovation can only happen when information is accessible and flows freely.

The implementation of social media can be one tool to break down barriers within corporations and/or between the organization and its environment. Social media is not the silver bullet; it's a means to create an open and collaborative culture. Twitter, blogs and wikis are just tools. Implementing them without an overall vision of collaboration is useless.

Culture and leadership are the most important factors of success for all organizations. Both are defined at the top — where collaboration and sharing need to be implemented as a vision. Without identifying the big picture, the organization will not be able to harness the full potential of social media.

A vision of collaboration and sharing guides an organization towards innovation. In this journey, social media is one of the tools that employees can utilize and help to bring the company vision to life. First, they must be empowered to explore new tools and ideas, share and even sometimes fail. There is no single way to use social media most effectively; it's diverse and personalized. People need to explore and develop their own best means within a given vision and direction.

Make people understand the power of sharing and collaboration and they will use social media in a way that benefits company success.

ERANIUM.POSTEROUS.com

Breaking Down the Fear of Social Media

Andrea Vascellari

After years spent in senior consulting what I find curious rather than surprising and what I still observe with interest is the unwillingness to change of organizations and executives. Finding arguments to facilitate the adoption of social media still remains an open challenge for many practitioners. Although it has the potential of making the difference, social media is often perceived by organizations as scary. So how can one work for the other?

The First Real Battle is Acceptance

The awareness of the change happening in our society must be followed by acceptance, which will consequentially translate into mindset shift and organizational change. The higher the degree of acceptance of change, the easier it will be to get the best out of it. If an organization is moving one step ahead it will be able to even anticipate the change — and you certainly don't need me to remind you of the great advantages of sitt ing at the bleeding edge within your industry, right?

The Role of Communicators

The only thing the executives understand is risk vs reward. There is a tendency to just look at risk only because they're afraid of losing control of the conversation or scared of being bashed publicly. Communicators have to give emphasis to the rewards that come with the adoption of social media and show how to contain, minimize and manage related risks. Most importantly communicators within organizations must change from order takers and become guides, advisors, coaches, conversation starters and creators of content that people want to talk about.

There's a Cultural Shift That Must Happen

I'm not talking about a revolution — social media can live well and be implemented within an organization's existing structure — but the communication needs to change. A CEO column written in full corporate jargon and posted on a website where comments are closed or censured can't be called a "blog." A recorded track of the quarterly meeting with a CFO reading numbers and unquestionably boring PowerPoint slides can't be called a "podcast" and published online.

Social Media is a Chance

It's an opportunity for a wide variety of internal and external communication improvements at different levels but if there's no way to talk to executives about it … Well perhaps their children or grandchildren will show them their iPhone and what they are doing with it. I'm sure something will change at that point!

ANDREAVASCELLARI.com

What Are You Waiting For?

Jeff Wallace

Ok, so you've heard about social media marketing. Congratulations. But what have you done to truly engage these approaches to benefit your business? If you're like most executives, the answer is *nothing*, or very little at best. Why is this? If you search for "social media marketing" on Google, you'll find over 127 million hits! How is someone supposed to figure this out with such immense amounts of information? In all the pandemonium surrounding social marketing, it's challenging to determine what makes sense. So what is one to do?

First, take a deep breath. Don't become overwhelmed by the enormity of information. There are those who have a great understanding of social marketing and its ins and outs. Surely, they can be invaluable resources. And, beyond having expertise, make sure they are able and willing to educate you and your business — that is, share their knowledge, not hoard it. Spending time sourcing these skilled individuals (vs scouring and attempting to digest the overabundance of information for the payback) is well worth it.

Next, understand that while social marketing may be relatively new, there are myriad tools that allow for designing, implementing, tracking and maintaining marketing campaigns. Of course, you could just fall victim to the belief that you must do something unique and innovative. But the reality is simply that you must do *something*.

Today's audiences are living within social networks, engaging in ways previously unavailable, and seeking recognition and communication from brands they choose in ways they desire. Don't spend time rationalizing how your audience is different than all others or why the methods used to reach audiences throughout the world won't work for yours. Rather, let those with the knowledge and experience help you design an approach that engages your respective audience and demonstrates your corporate desire to engage them on their terms. And, rather than seeking distinctiveness in the tools you employ, see uniqueness and relevance in the way you integrate these tools in compelling ways to generate business benefit.

Finally, do as you've always done … monitor, track and adjust accordingly. Through proper trialing, you will find success in reaching your audiences within today's social networks. You will engage existing and new audience members. You will create new and desired communication channels with your customers and other relevant stakeholders. Finally, you will be surprised by the results.

So, stop waiting … it's time to get busy!

LINKEDIN.com/in/jeffwallace913

Seven Simple Ways to Ignite Conversations and Boost Employee Loyalty with Video

Thomas R. Clifford

Every company wants to attract prospects and engage their customers, right? That's why so many companies take advantage of video. Video is compelling. It ignites conversations. It boosts brand loyalty.

That's all well and good, of course. But hey, did you know companies can use video internally for the same reasons? To ignite conversations that matter most to employees? And build employee loyalty? That's right. So what are you waiting for?

Here are seven simple ways your organization can use video to ignite employee conversations and boost employee loyalty.

1. Meaning

People want to contribute and to make a difference. In a tough economy, meaningful work becomes increasingly important. Grab your camera. Film employees who understand how their work fits within the big picture.

2. Leadership

Who are the leaders? Why are they leaders? What do they do all day? How do they affect what people do? What makes them tick? Start capturing the humanity behind the ivory tower. This can start reducing employees' fears and doubts while slowly building trust.

3. Trust

Imagine the outcomes of Formula One racing teams if they didn't have high levels of trust. In a word — disastrous. The same applies to your team. When trust is high, performance goes up. Go capture trust in action. Show what high-trust teams look like. Show the outcomes of high-trust actions and behaviors. Film it. Show it. Share it.

4. Passion

What drives someone to be passionate? What's their secret sauce? Find passionate employees. Talk to them. Interview them. Record their story. Edit their story by themes. Then create several short segments so employees can understand what drives them to succeed.

5. Volunteerism

Are there employees who are changing the world? Are they making life a little bit better for someone? Do other employees know about it? Pack the camera. Leave the cubicle. Show employees making a difference.

6. Purpose

Do employees really know the goals of the company? Is everyone clear on what the top priorities are? Capture short stories featuring teams executing goals. Be specific. Show one priority per video.

7. Success

Success breeds success. Where are your success stories? Don't keep them a secret! Stephen Covey calls these success stories "islands of success." Tap into these "islands of success" so others can learn from their experiences.

DIRECTORTOM.com

Human Business Design

Uwe Hook
llllllllllllllllllllllllllll

Humans believe to be rational, self-guided and controlled creatures. This thinking has led to the Great Recession with all its implications. Wall Street, dominated by numbers and highly-educated number crunchers and intellectuals, should have been the perfect playground for rational decisions. That playground has disappeared. But what happened to all the other playgrounds of rational thinking: enterprises, institutions and organizations? And where do C-level executives go from here?

Let's face the truth: All of us are much more Homer than Mr. Spock. But we've based our organizational structures on left brain thinking: Organized, structured and optimized. Just like our basements, brains and desks, right?

Right!

For businesses to succeed post-connectedness revolution, enterprises have to change every aspect of their business and their industry. We have approached the end of the left brain potential and need to connect with the right side by developing a collaborative and co-creative ecosystem that includes all stakeholders. This ecosystem has to co-create value outside of shareholder and market demands. Way outside. Enterprises have to focus on ideas that live within their products and services and expand on them to develop bigger ideas. And a better world to live in.

To achieve this audacious goal, organizations have to adopt a hybrid top-down and bottoms-up approach. Executives have to direct their team to focus less on internal competition and more on internal/external collaboration. Barriers have to be broken down, silos eradicated. In addition, executives need to identify highly connected and socially versatile individuals and empower them as change agents. These change agents will spread the benefits of co-creation virally through the organization, transforming businesses from containers of outdated values into industry change agents.

All this can't be done through mission statements, strategy sessions or CEO memos. It has to be implemented human by human, day-by-day, step-by-step. Corporations need to forget about their own wants and needs, focusing on the needs and desires of all of their stakeholders. A healthy ecosystem feeds on itself without much supervision and intervention. The current ecosystem needs stringent rules, rigid management and a disregard of the human spirit. Transformative businesses will be based on humanity and the spirit of collaboration. Based on Human Business Design.

llllllllllllllllllllllllllllllllllllllllllllllllllllllllllllllllllllllllllllllllllllllllll
CONVERSATIONAGENCY.WORDPRESS.com

Connect, Start the Conversation

Lynae Johnson

It all started with an invitation to join LinkedIn. New to the social media scene, I asked my boss if joining was worthwhile, to which he answered an emphatic, "Yes." Not long after, I was hooked. Why? It is social. This sounds like an oxymoron; however, within corporate life each individual has professional and personal goals. Communicating on a personal level through social networking lets you into people's lives, allowing you to understand more about them and their company.

Sales is education. When I was a child my career aspirations were to be a Mom and a teacher. I am both, although I don't have a classroom of 27 fourth graders; my classroom is my client base and potential client base. Yes, ultimately I take home a paycheck because my clients make purchases; however, if they aren't making an educated decision then I have failed them.

This ties into social networking through educating yourself about your client. Connect with them. Let them know you are human and recognize that they are human as well. By connecting at this level you learn about their habits, the needs of their company and ultimately their connections as well. This builds confidence and loyalty in you and your product. And let's face it; it's enjoyable.

Where to begin connecting socially? Start with one application and get comfortable, then move on to the next. Different people enjoy different methods of communication, and you will find they often compliment each other. Blogging was very daunting until I began to brainstorm topics; I found that it was a really easy vehicle to address common client concerns while relaying our companies' values.

My anthem is an oldie; treat your clients how you want to be treated. I know this is easy to say, but walking the walk is also easy. The more you connect with your clients and learn *how* you can help them, the more successful they will be. In turn you are successful.

Just don't forget your colleagues; tools they find useful in specific applications you may find valuable as well. Including colleagues and communicating with them through social media shows your clients that you are unified. As you are learning more about your clients, you will also pick up new ideas and methods along the way. Then everyone wins!

TRADESHOW-STUFF.com

Corporate Conversations

Priyanka Sachar

The moment we think of Facebook, the image of people playing Farmville, Mafia Wars or poking each other comes to mind. When we think of LinkedIn, we picture people furiously trying to find new jobs. Picturing Twitter could range from people giving minute details of their lives to chatting as if they are on IM steroids. It is difficult to imagine any effective usage of work hours from these visions.

Those are the reasons why most corporates ban social networking sites. However, very few realize the actual benefits it can give them. Apart from the definite advantages that incorporating social media officially can bring to an organization there are many disadvantages that *not* implementing it can cause.

Take a look at the case of an agency person who went to FedEx, Memphis to give a presentation on digital media, ending up criticizing that city and earning the wrath of the client, putting himself in the very situation that he, of all people, should have known how to avoid. Or one can take a look at the waiter who tweeted about a celebrity not paying up for her meal, not giving a tip and ending up getting fired for not showing discretion to a client.

It is recommended to "allow" controlled usage of social networks by having a clear cut "Social Media Usage Policy." In these times, we are very much judged by what we write on the internet. It holds true for individuals as well as organizations. Perceptions matter.

Corporates need to realize that social media, if implemented correctly within the organization, can also extend various benefits to their brand reach and offer engagement to a bigger audience. What is better than all employees taking on the task of a PR agency! For doing this correctly, motivation in the right form, branding standards awareness, educating teams about what is acceptable to the organisation and what is not, the terms the organization would like to associate with or never associate with, are some of the necessary steps.

At the same time it is necessary to take care that one doesn't stifle employees with too many do's/don'ts. Corporates usually have legal departments approving every word that goes to the external world, but social media doesn't work that way. All you need is a canned, made up act and you push yourself far away from what you set out to achieve. A well-crafted social media policy would allow social media usage and also take care that employees remain productive by using it as a healthy mix of personal usage along with careful usage of being the mouthpieces of the organization.

BLOG.TWILIGHTFAIRY.in
DELHIBLOGGERSBLOC.com

Business Marketing and the Social Imperative

Michael O'Toole

Business marketers have never had the budgets or spotlight of our B2C colleagues. We operate in the world of niche targets, sophisticated decision-makers and complex purchase processes. Marketing that doesn't look like sales enablement has always been a tough sell.

And so it is with social media. Business marketers who want to go social face a litany of objections: "social media is really a consumer play — show me a success story that isn't Zappos, Best Buy or Comcast" or "our clients don't care what we had for breakfast, and certainly don't want to hear us Tweeting about it."

If you're a business marketer waiting on the social media sidelines, you want two key questions answered before you dive in.

Why Bother?

Your customers are already participating. You already have fans — and foes — of your company talking about you. Set up a Google alert or search a Twitter hash tag for your product brands. You'll get the unvarnished conversation in a hurry. The good news? Buyers want you involved in the conversation. Recent research by Toolbox.com/PJA shows that vendors are a welcome presence in IT social networks.

How, Exactly, Do I Get Started?

There are a million ways to get involved in social media, and most don't involve sending tweets to your clients. Apply social strategies in very practical ways to support critical objectives that you already own. Here are two to try this year.

Use social media to frame the conversation for new products. Pick an important product release in the upcoming year, and choose one key buying audience who needs to be convinced. The task is to explain how your solution addresses problems they care about. Think beyond the white paper. Short (yes, 140 characters could be a start), interesting (lose the sales pitch), and frequent is the goal. Next, syndicate content to all channels where the audience congregates: LinkedIn groups, your Web site, third-party community sites. Slideshare. Don't ignore Facebook (check out the McKinsey Quarterly Fan page for a best practice) or YouTube (look up the Autodesk channel).

Use social strategies to improve event effectiveness. Use social media — content, viral contests, and pre-event networking — to drive attendance and post-show engagement. Check out the 2009 Forrester Groundswell Award winners in the "Energizing" category for great examples by Sonic Foundry and IBM.

The most important question to answer is, "What do I get out of it?" The companies referenced above drive customer acquisition and build enviable brand loyalty through social marketing. Social media, practiced well, can lift the veil between you and your customers, and bring out your best, most collaborative instincts.

MPDAILYFIX.com/contributors/mike_otoole/posts.html

Corporate Culture: A Social Media Killer

Pete Jones

IIIIIIIIIIIIIIIIIIIIIIIIIIIIII

It is no question large corporate companies have failed to fully embrace social media like many of their smaller peers. Actually, this trend is not unique to social media — large corporations have failed to adapt a number of new innovative measures.

A great illustration of large corporation's failure to adapt and utilize social media is detailed in a recent poll by a local employer. That poll asked employees, "How often do you read 'blogs' on the internet?" Only 47 percent of nearly 5,000 employees never read a blog. Another 27 percent rarely frequent blogs. This particular employer also strongly *suggested* against access to blogs or social media during the work day, a fact that has to weigh very strongly on their employees' understanding of the medium. The sample group in this poll was small, but it provides a good illustration of the overall majority and further illustrates corporate employees do not get their information from blogs.

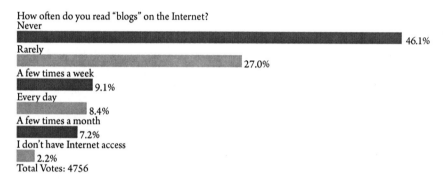

How often do you read "blogs" on the Internet?
Never
46.1%
Rarely
27.0%
A few times a week
9.1%
Every day
8.4%
A few times a month
7.2%
I don't have Internet access
2.2%
Total Votes: 4756

There are many reasons corporations fail to interact on the social media realm, mainly because social media is not a measurable statistic that can be reported to stakeholders. Corporations must also consider the legality and risk of allowing employees to essentially "speak" to their customers. Large corporations have failed to fully understand that social media is not about one way communication, like traditional marketing. Customer conversations on social media platforms provide corporations direct access and a unique medium to interact with and discuss products. The conversations are already happening, it is time for corporations to embrace the medium and take the next steps to incorporate it into their business plan.

Imagine if corporations allowed their employees the ability to utilize social media platforms at work. Think of all the sets of ears listening to brand conversations and providing timely feedback to management. Corporations would have a medium to their customers that would trump traditional media. Corporations still hide behind the ever popular "network security" excuse and limit employee's involvement on social media websites. Guess we'll just have to let the small guys gain market share with their hip and innovative customer conversations.

Twitter Has Not Jumped the Shark

Morriss Partee

Twitter went mainstream in the Spring of 2009. That's when traditional media personalities like Oprah Winfrey, Ashton Kutcher, and CNN jumped on the Twitter train. Many established Twitter veterans decried that being overrun by these bandwagon-jumpers would portend the end of Twitter as they knew it. Some wailed "send out the search parties for the next Twitter!" and "now that THEY'RE on twitter, *we're* outta here!"

But such short-sighted proclamations entirely miss the point of how the world is now networked. It does not matter that Oprah, Ashton, or CNN are on Twitter if you don't care about them. No one, including celebrities, has to be a part of *your* Twitter experience.

The reason why Twitter has had difficulty scaling its platform to accommodate the millions of new users flooding into the Twittersphere is that Twitter is *not* one giant network, but rather millions of individual, customized networks. And that requires great computing horsepower to operate. *Your* Twitter network is completely under your control. If you don't want to read what someone has to say on Twitter (or Facebook, or any other networking site), then simply don't follow that person.

On many occasions, I've heard business people ask, "What's the next Twitter?" or "What's the next Facebook?" These questions reveal their belief that they don't have to jump in now, they *shouldn't* jump in now, because there will be something new right around the corner. The executive doesn't want to expend unnecessary resources to be in MySpace, only to have Facebook come along and all but usurp its relevance.

My answer to those folks: "You're not asking the right question." These are the same people who asked, "What is the next world wide web?" back in the late 1990s. I knew, even then, that that was the wrong question. The question ought to have been "Where is the web going?" or "What are the developing trends in the web as we know it today?" With hindsight, we can see that dynamic, social web sites became more popular than static sites, but there was no "next web."

Today, the question companies should be asking is not, "What's the *next* Twitter?" but instead "How do we make the most of *today's* social media and networking tools?"

If companies pay attention to what is here right now, they will also discover what's next as it unfolds before their eyes.

EVERYTHINGCU.WORDPRESS.com

The End of the Campaign

Hugh de Winton

We tend to treat campaigns as having a start and end date because that's easiest for us, it's how we've always operated, and it's the context that the Board understand marketing should be in. We're in control and we'll dictate how active we are and the crowd will respond accordingly. Once the campaign finishes, we'll sit around, try and work out if it worked and put it forward for a few awards if the statistics look impressive.

The problem is, we're no longer operating in a context where the brand dictates the situation. It's a collaborative, increasingly digital, realtime environment where ideas can spread like lightening if they're remarkable enough or flop horrendously. As important as the idea that is immediately put out, how the people whom it reached react to it is more important; what they do with it, if it resonates — from here on in an infinite number of things can happen, this should be the fun bit for the brand but instead it's perceived a something uncontrollable.

How can we still call this chaos the campaign? We can't, the idea is out there, it's being passed around and there is no way you can put an end date on it. The traditional definition of the campaign is dead within two way brand communication. This should be a cause for celebration.

In the real world, people have identities and rarely change them, they live in beta, trying stuff, working out what suits. If a brand was a person, it would be wearing a flat cap and tweed to one party and then rock up two months later having not seen anyone wearing a string vest and talking in a new accent. Being at every party isn't necessary. I don't go to them all (some look crap on Facebook) but I do just try to relax, get a few beers in and actually provide a bit of fun for the people around me, I also never go AWOL. If brands moved away from campaigns and behaved like the rest of us, they might start to understand how to be truly social.

HUGHDEWINTON.BLOGSPOT.com

In the Boardroom

Experimentation Is the Mother of Survival

Joseph Jaffe

In 2009, I wrote an article for *Adweek*, one of the leading US marketing trade publications, titled, "2009: The Year of Nothing." In the piece I challenged marketers to innovate and specifically experiment, even amidst the current economic recession and over all, risk-averse climate.

While the corporate boardroom continues to fixate on short-term results and specifically, quarterly earnings, it would appear that the very people who keep us in business, namely our customers, are living their lives at a diametrically opposed place.

And all the while they are pulling further and further ahead, we are falling further and further behind.

If marketing is a commitment and not a campaign, how are we committing ourselves to our lifeblood: our customers? Our employees? What kinds of quality relationships are we establishing, nurturing and building over time? Or are we just remaining on the sidelines; watching; waiting for something to happen, hoping or even praying for someone else to make the first move. The sad truth of the matter is that our wish will most likely be granted by our competitors and the result may be our obliteration from this earth.

It's not good enough to be average. It's not good enough to be part of the chasing pack. Every moment of hesitation has the potential to be cataclysmic in terms of the impact on our business and brand. If it is true that *he who hesitates is lost*, then surely the time to act is now. Time is not on our side. Advancements in technology, coupled with a rapidly evolving consumer have accelerated and compressed the lifecycle and death spiral associated with competitive advancements, in-roads and differentiation.

Whether you find yourself in the heart of the "perfect storm" or its eye (as in it may *appear* to be calm, but your sense of security is a false one) of new consumerism, democratization of control, decision-making and influence, and leveling of playing fields, I'd like to give you this singular piece of advice:

Innovate now. And do it while you can, before you have to.

Carve out a separate and dedicated budget towards innovation and experimentation. Attempt to execute a realistic number of experiments in 2010. Perhaps your magic number is three. Or perhaps it's four (one per quarter). Be prepared to make mistakes. In other words, failure with a purpose (and that purpose being learning) is really not failure at all.

Above all, in 12 months from now, do not dare to be in a position where you look back and realize you accomplished nothing. Because if you do, you may once and for all, have fallen so far behind, that catching up will be well and truly impossible.

Go!

JAFFEJUICE.com

Association Board Briefing: Confronting the End of Membership as We Know It

Jeff De Cagna

Associations are at the beginning of a profound shift in the nature and demands of stakeholder relations and voluntary engagement driven primarily by the inescapable realities of a web-enabled world.

Association boards of directors must challenge themselves, staff and other leaders to engage in serious experimentation and learning about possible futures by identifying ways to capitalize on three emerging dynamics that challenge the sustainability of the current association membership model.

1. **Meaning is the business case** — in today's "reset" economy, busy and tired association stakeholders are reflecting on what matters most, and allocating their limited discretionary time and attention accordingly. In this context, relevance is a losing argument for associations. Instead, associations must help their current and future stakeholders nurture a deeper connection to an inspiring organizational purpose, and support stakeholder efforts to make meaning around issues of personal and professional significance.

2. **Social is a way of being** — The dramatic growth of public social networks such as Facebook and Twitter confirms the commitment of people everywhere to on-going social exchange. We want to connect with others, no matter where they are, to share information, access ideas and find inspiration. Over the course of this last decade, social technologies have helped to renew our understanding of the word "social" itself. No longer is it merely a descriptor of an organized group activity or a set of personal attributes. Today, we recognize "social" as a holistic interface, a way of being in the world that is more generative than simply being a member.

3. **Contribution is king** — social technologies also challenge traditional notions of association participation. Conventional volunteerism, built on a foundation of formal, centralized and narrowly focused roles within the organizational hierarchy, is giving way to a more open, collaborative and highly distributed structure of voluntary engagement that happens whenever and wherever necessary. Going forward, many of the most important association contributors likely will not be members, but the passionate and committed stakeholders who find the greatest simplicity and meaning in their experience of engagement.

We are witnessing the end of the association membership model as we know it, and association boards must act decisively to figure out what comes next. Boards must lead the effort to confront and question old assumptions, unleash original thinking and champion genuine innovation. **This leaves only one final question: is your association's board ready to answer the call to 21st century leadership?**

PRINCIPLEDINNOVATION.com

In the Boardroom

Adam Joseph

Contrary to popular belief, the dinosaurs didn't become extinct 65 million years ago. Many disguised themselves with grey hair and suits and have been surviving in the boardrooms of major corporations to this day.

Recent analysis by risk management experts RiskMetrics revealed the average age of directors in the boardroom is currently 59 (see http://bit.ly/8Krqjx). Rupert Murdoch (my boss, no dinosaur) made a famous speech back in 2005 where he coined the terms "digital natives" and "digital immigrants" (see the full speech at http://bit.ly/6ecqrQ).

Fast-forward to 2010 and I believe we need to add a new group when it comes to many CEOs and boards — "Digital Exiles." Digital Exiles are here against their will. They are control freaks in a world of empowered consumers, reluctantly being forced to join the conversation. They are old-school risk managers in a world where staff can all too easily get themselves and their employer in big trouble through social media (see http://bit.ly/4Oa3bZ).

But I'm being a bit unfair here.

A lot of CEOs and C-suite executives do "get it." And while few may have personal Facebook profiles, a fair number can be found on LinkedIn. While a tiny minority spend any time blogging, most appreciate "opinion leaders." A miniscule number are tweeting, but many have heard of it (see http://bit.ly/5lYItZ).

Why is any of this important?

Because I personally believe that to really "get" social media you have to personally get stuck into it. Not second-nature for 60-year old board members.   So that's social media *In the Boardroom*. But what about social media <u>marketing</u>? This was always going to be a hard sell to C-suite executives.

Marketing has a tough enough time as is in the boardroom, justifying its existence as an investment rather than a cost (see http://bit.ly/8FN6Rl). The trick to pitching social media marketing is to talk the same language as the Board, which means credible marketing metrics. Marketers will get the contempt they deserve if they rant about "fans," "friends" and "followers."

Yong Fook wrote an excellent presentation, Social Media ROI, which urged marketers to ignore meaningless metrics (see http://bit.ly/7PXhQ8). Success metrics should be defined that are relevant to your business. For example, online sales — Dell on Twitter (see http://bit.ly/4ne0oH); offline sales — JC Penny's *In the Doghouse* viral on YouTube (see http://bit.ly/8GTh99); global publicity value — Tourism Queensland's *Best Job in the World* and so on.

In fact, the most exciting thing about social media is there are so many other great case studies yet to be created, from campaigns yet to be conceived.

When it comes to social media in the boardroom — money talks, conversation walks.

LINKEDIN.com/in/adamjoseph

A Social Brand Needs a Bold CEO

Steve Sponder

For organizations to be successful in this new hyper-word-of-mouth world, they will need to fully embrace the notion of a building a social brand.

A social brand is one that is able to excel in three core areas; it can actively listen, it has appropriate social behavior and it is able to build win-win relationships with its stakeholders.

Active listening is required if the brand is to truly be part of the market conversations, being part of the conversation provides valuable insight and critical feedback. Without active listening, and appropriate responses, the brand is still operating in the pre-social media world of mass communication.

Appropriate social behavior is the easiest to define — authentic, honest, transparent, human — but it's the hardest to successfully implement. Ultimately it will come down to the organization's commitment to a social brand value system and a people strategy that is aligned to this.

Lastly, win-win relationships are about the value exchange between the brand and each of its stakeholders: prospects, customers, employees, influencers, investors, etc. This value can take different forms, so for customers it could be about the performance of the product, the quality of the customer support or the influence they may have over shaping the product development.

In reality, the impending challenges to re-engineer an organisation in order to be able to successfully build a social brand is huge; aligning internal departments, processes and communication channels is just the tip of the iceberg.

The conclusion, therefore, is that the only way an organization can effectively meet these challenges will be if the board, and more specifically the CEO, genuinely understands this new social world, is committed to building a social brand, has a clear, effective strategy and strong leadership to make it happen.

There is certainly an opportunity for organizations to get a competitive edge by building social brands although the interesting question is how organizations will differentiate themselves in the future when all brands are social brands.

BLOG.STEVESPONDER.com

Put "Say Thank You" On Your Social Media To-Do List

Michael E. Rubin

What gets your highest priority on the daily social media to-do list? Responding to a customer service complaint from Twitter? Answering a prospect's question on your corporate Facebook page? Writing a post for your corporate blog?

Here is the answer: none of the above. Instead, start by saying "thank you."

Social media makes it amazingly easy to communicate directly with fans, partners, customers, and prospects, but we sometimes forget that the easiest way to start or continue a conversation is to express thanks. It astonishes me to see so many brands seemingly ignore their fans and customers by neglecting to say thank you.

Five Ways to Put "Thank You" on Your Corporate Social Media To-Do List

I recommend putting "Say thank you" on your corporate social media daily to-do list. Here are five ways to do that:

1. When someone leaves a comment on your blog (positive or negative), say thank you. They gave you some of their own precious attention, so you should take the time to say thank you.

2. When someone sends you a tweet or replies to one of your own, use the @reply function in Twitter to reply to them.

3. Your customers (both existing and prospective) often have plenty of advice for your company. If one of them provides something for you — an introduction, a key insight, or a pat on the back — write a thank you note. It costs almost nothing, but the gesture will return a great deal.

4. If a customer leaves a note about your company, service, or product on a message board, send a note via email saying, "Thank you." If the commentary is negative, say "We heard you" and offer to help fix the problem.

5. Block out ten minutes of your workday to search and reply to comments and tweets.

Take the time to say thank you. Put it on your corporate social media daily to-do list. Doing so opens the door to generating a conversation, strengthening customer loyalty, and ultimately, creating positive word of mouth.

EMPOWERMM.POSTEROUS.com

Social? My Agency Does That

Jon Burg

|||||||||||||||||||||||||||

Social media is exciting. Social media holds tremendous business potential, much of it as-yet untapped and certainly untracked or properly attributed. But does social media demand or deserve a seat in the boardroom?

The decision to add a Chief Social Officer to your C-suite should not be taken lightly, especially in corporations of scale. I would recommend considering the following two filters:

1. Is social media core to your equity statement?

   If your corporation relies heavily on collaboration, innovation and communications positioning, you will likely require a strong social strategy. Advisors and agencies can help build the necessary infrastructures, solutions and policy, but I would think twice before outsourcing core equity without strong executive management.

2. How socially ready is your business?

   The culture of your business defines your social readiness. Does your C-suite enjoy feedback and conversations with employees and lower tier customers? Honestly, are your business units rock solid silos or does everyone play nicely in the sandbox? Is your number one goal customer and employee satisfaction, or is this just a "nice to have" that may or may not show up on the quarterly balance sheets? Is your business built on an honest, real passion? Do your employees really feel this passion? Does your corporate culture embody this passion?

The Case For a Social Champion

Regardless of whether or not he or she has a seat in your boardroom, every corporation needs a social champion and an executive sponsor to see to the inevitable challenges this champion will face. This champion needs to have defined goals, broad access, strong executive support and work across nearly every capability in your company. This champion will likely need a supporting cast, nearly all of whom can be borrowed from other business units (this will also help drive efficient change utilizing existing resources). This champion will lead the charge for social policy internally and externally, collaboration internally, social cultural change in both internal and external communications, manage agency relationships and maintain consistency across all communications and campaigns. The workplace is changing and your customers' buying influences are evolving — It would be foolish to move forward without a knowledgeable, strategic social champion.

Social is about more than a campaign or a communications policy. It's about the culture of your corporation and your philosophy of business. If you have skin in the game, you owe it to yourself to build for success.

|||||||||||||||||||||||||||||||||||||||||||||||||||||||||||||||||||||

JBURG.TYPEPAD.com/future

One Million Acts of Green

Cory Coley-Christakos

Start with an extraordinary idea. Such is Willa Black's advice for getting your organization to embrace social media. As VP, Corporate Affairs at Cisco Canada, that's exactly what Willa did when she brought "One Million Acts of Green" to Cisco's executive team.

What began as a unique branding concept transformed into a movement, and a vibrant social network of Canadians who rallied together with a common purpose — save the planet, one green act at a time.

The Right Idea

At the outset, Willa's main premise was that any social media campaign they developed had to be interesting enough that someone would pass it on. She wanted a program that would excite people, and incite them to action. "It's one thing to show your brand to someone, it's another to engage them. It's one thing to bring people to your website, it's another to have them want to get involved."

Combining two very current themes, social media and environmental sustainability, "One Million Acts of Green" was an idea so remarkable that everyone at Cisco caught the spirit ... *eventually.*

Perseverance

While her boss "got it" right away, Willa spent months aligning internal support for the program, starting locally, tapping into the power base, ensuring the key decision-makers were onside, and addressing concerns about risk. Each person she converted from sceptic to supporter became invested in the program's success.

Cultural Alignment

It helped that the concept of social media fit perfectly with Cisco's culture and overall marketing umbrella — "the human network effect." It also helped that the underlying cause was exceptionally worthy.

Emotional Engagement

None of this was enough to make the investment a slam-dunk. Willa had to inspire the imagination of Cisco's executive team, which she did with these words: "If we do it right, this is the way to rally a nation."

Transformational Results

The idea galvanized media, celebrities, corporations and communities. Canadians logged 1.8 million individual acts of green on the "Facebook-style" website, and saved 106 million kilograms of greenhouse gases, before the movement went global (see onemillionactsofgreen.com).

For Cisco, this meant a 479 percent spike in media hits, seven awards, a highly positive brand impact, and doors opened to new partnerships, new customers, and new conversations.

Naturally, these exceptional results would not have been possible without a full 360° strategy, nimble execution and plenty of hard work, but it all started with one extraordinary idea and the will to make it a reality.

LINKEDIN.com/in/corycoleychristakos

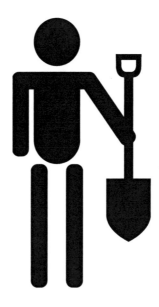

Innovation and Execution

||||||||||||||||||||||||||||||||||||||||||||||||||||||||||||||||||||||||||||||||||||||||||||||||||||||||||||||||||||||||||||||

Innovation and Execution

Sam Ismail

Innovation is a term bandied about with alarming regularity like "visionary," "creativity" and other now-smoldering embers of language that once carried much weight but have been marginalized over time through equal measures of misuse and misunderstanding.

It is strangely fitting then that true innovation is an ever-elusive beast to practitioners in the dark arts of communications. How to innovate, and the reasons why, as an industry, we struggle to innovate with any consistency, can be gleaned by delving into the etymology of the word itself. "Innovate" comes from the Latin *innovare* (to renew, or alter) which comes from *novus* which means "new".

Therein lies the crux of innovation. New. The lifeblood of being able to create and execute innovative solutions. It is unfortunate then, that there is a patently obvious lack of anything *new* in an alarming number of organizations within the communications industry.

We recruit from the same pool of people, citing issues of "cultural fit." We value efficiency over brilliance and conformity over rebellion. To further shroud innovation in a cloak of mediocrity, we look to each other for praise and criticism, forgetting that it is the success of our clients that we should be most concerned about. We don't design communications for client profit, but for awards and plaudits from our elitist circle of professionals.

This cycle of self-referentialism only euthanizes our ability to provide fresh perspective. This behavior has permeated our thinking so deeply that we even dress identically. The next time you are unfortunate enough to attend an advertising awards show, observe the number of black shirts and black dresses in attendance. The irony of course, is that those in said shirts and dresses claim to be among the most creative on the planet.

What is the cure? As is often the case with complex issues, the solution is simple. Break out of the cycle of sameness we have all constructed around us. Observe those you wish to affect everywhere you can find them. Be relentless in digesting every experience they digest. Understand what they hate, what they love, what they want to make better. Then, make it better and genuinely change the fabric of their day to day existence. Not for an hour, a day or even a week, but forever. In that place you will find ideas that are new and terrifying.

That place will be innovation.

SAMISMAIL.com

Get Off Your Ass

Brian Reich

Our society has changed dramatically. We talk about it all the time, in the context of business (flattening), media (speeding up), and community (connecting). But it's even bigger than that.

Technology and the internet have given us greater control over what information we get and share, how we spend our time, and to whom we are connected. We are more diverse as a society, more informed as individuals, and more involved as communities. We have the tools, the connections, the access at our fingertips — and thus are empowered as never before to do something incredible.

But we aren't.

Because we can use the tools that are now widely available online to conduct campaigns, send notices, and raise awareness of issues — more efficiently and cost effectively than ever before — we have lost sight of what real impact looks like and how success should be measured. We've settled for low open rates for emails and names on an email list as signs of progress — instead of demanding more from our leaders, and ourselves.

Think about it this way — the internet has made us lazy. Too much attention has been paid to the process of making our government more transparent, our political campaigns more bottom-up, our marketing more audience-driven, and our media more participatory. Not enough consideration has been given to whether or not the big issues are being addressed, the bad behaviors are being changed, and the issues that plague our society are being solved.

They aren't.

We need a reset. We don't need a plan — that's too short term, we need to think bigger/broader. We don't need a model — we have never done what we need to do now, so there isn't anything to emulate. We don't need a strategy — this isn't about developing some roadmap or building a campaign. We need a total, complete, top-to-bottom, reset. We need to change the way we think, act, organize. We need to change how we talk, and listen. Everything we know, and how it is applied, must be reconsidered and re-applied.

Truly, anything is possible in today's age, so it's time we throw out the old playbook and tried something entirely new. Hit reset. Use the potential the internet and technology offer to truly change the world.

There is no time to waste. Get off your ass.

THINKINGABOUTMEDIA.com

The Marketing of Innovation

Cam Beck

Imagine being introduced to someone who is claimed to be "the future of your company" and full of "innovative" ideas. The problem is that you've never heard his name before, and you don't even like the person who introduces you.

"I've got some great ideas," the new guy exhorts, before he prattles off a few dozen thoughts without as much as taking a breath.

"Innovative. Sure," your conscience scoffs. "What good is innovation if I can't make any money with it?"

So immediately you're skeptical, and you do your best to purge your mind of the drivel that is coming out of his mouth. After all, the guy looks like he slept in his clothes, he's not speaking in a language you understand, and you find his idealistic exuberance to be somewhat annoying.

As he continues, you clench your teeth behind your smile, prohibited by social norms from expressing your true contempt. Your eyes dart around the room, looking for someone else to pass this blowhard on to, so you can go about doing the same thing you've been doing every day for the last twenty-five years.

Detecting no interest from you, the stranger looks somewhat dejected. "Well, I'll see you later. Maybe." As he walks off, you get a sense of satisfaction for "sticking it" to the guy who just tried to ruin your day with all of his crazy ideas.

"Maybe," you think to yourself, hopefully, as you breathe a sigh of relief, "I'll never have to see that guy again."

Just then, your boss comes up to you and says, "I saw you talking to our customer." Your eyes widen as panic swells in the pit of your gut. He continues, "I'm dying to ask. What did he say?"

***

The first step in executing an innovative idea is to be aware of what transcendent need your company helps your customers fill.

If you do that, you will be less likely to assume that, just because they use social media, they'll flock to whatever "branded" tripe you build. They aren't in it for the tactics — no one but marketers care about tactics — and they have no interest in "engaging" with your brand.

But they are out there, and they are talking. Next time, show a little respect. Listen.

CHAOSSCENARIO.com

Extreme Foreignness, Innovation and Execution

C.B. Whittemore

Opportunities for innovation surround us. Yet, we don't always recognize them. Why not? I believe, because we shut ourselves off from them. Some of it has to do with so much doom and gloom that we've squashed our intellectual curiosity; some, with not having figured out how to manage the information chaos both personally and corporately; and some, with not being sure how to explore, experiment and exchange ideas. How to stop shutting out innovation?

Imagine that you are American and have been sent on assignment to Tokyo. You may admire Japanese culture, but you can neither speak the language nor read Kanji. What then?

Will you opt to seek out others just like you, perhaps through the American Consulate? Will you limit interactions to fellow expats, live within an American compound, send your children to an American school and do your best to purchase only American-like foods?

Or, will you open yourself to full foreign immersion: walk the streets, listen for patterns, observe body language, go to local Yakitori BBQ joints and ride the subway? Take Japanese language classes and find bilingual sherpas with whom to bridge the cultural and language barriers and engage in conversation to make sense of the differences? Pretty soon, you reach a point where you are able to participate fully in the experience and are already considering new integrated approaches.

I equate innovation with the experience of extreme foreignness. Not that you have to go all the way to Tokyo. Rather, by opening yourself up to conversation and the variety of perspectives that conversation uncovers, you open the door to innovation — to hearing about customer frustrations and suggestions for improvement. That's what Fiskars has done with its brand ambassadors, the Fiskateers, who provide feedback on products and obtain insights from retailers and consumers.

Conversation can also help ensure better execution. Take Wiggly Wigglers and its crowdsourced catalog. What better way to engage customers and community by executing as a result of conversation-based innovation!

The best part of these types of conversation based innovations is that they lead to continuous improvement; to small successes that build one on the other and that enable you to rapidly become fluent in what one was a total foreign language and culture.

Are you ready for a dose of extreme foreignness?

SIMPLEMARKETINGBLOG.com

In the BRICs... Where Innovation Is Emerging

John Rosen

Just arrived at the airport in some god-forsaken third world cesspool, er, BRIC, where my client (a big and well-known company) had directed me to work face-to-face with their in-country personnel, I was, unfortunately, engaged in the supremely unrewarding task of texting my wholly unresponsive American-based client (the human, who had flown in on a separate flight) in hopes that we could share a cab to the hotel.

- Why was it so unrewarding to be texting the client?
- Why was I in this country in the first place?
- Why couldn't we just handle all this with webinars, email, text messages, shared files or wikis, etc?

The unavoidably depressing answer was that the client (the human) who is approximately twelve years younger than I, didn't "… understand all that newfangled e-stuff." Seriously. Early in the engagement, which required amassing tons of data, we set up a shared site for use by the entire project team. About 15 people on three different payrolls were able to access the site with no problem; he could not.

"Can't you just make me a disk?" was the request. I sighed.

What I promptly discovered was that real commercialization innovation is occurring in these markets precisely because they are *emerging*. Their governments have invested billions in mobile and broadband technology — millions of connections and, mercifully, few credit cards. I saw a variety of ideas in execution for such things as phone-to-phone payments, downloading e-cash along with data, refilling prepaid cards anywhere in the world, etc. For example, assume you want to buy a pair of shoes. You can now, using only your phone:

- Tweet your friends about the idea
- Send them a photo
- Get them (more likely, your significant other) to approve the idea
- Notify your bank
- Download e-cash directly to your phone
- Swipe the phone at the shoe store for payment for this one transaction (this is all absurdly secure and password-protected at about three thousand levels, don't ask)
- Send another photo of how hot you look in the shoes
- Call a cab and go home, or, more likely, out to dinner with the significant other

No credit cards, no cash, no waiting around, just transacting in record time while sharing the experience with your friends. In the BRICS. Where the commercialization of e-innovation is occurring.

Innovation Is Overrated

David Berkowitz

Who doesn't love innovation? That's what gets you the fame, the babes, the chapter in the history books, and — most importantly — a few minutes on the hit American TV show "Shark Tank."

Yet most of marketing, including conversational marketing, isn't innovation. It's not supposed to be. If innovation was all that mattered, there'd only be one great corporate blog, and then the rest wouldn't matter. There'd only be one well constructed Facebook page for a brand, and maybe one breakthrough engagement ad on Facebook's homepage. There would just be one marketer using Twitter for customer service in a way that changed their organization, and one more marketer tying feedback from Twitter to their research and development cycle.

No, innovation doesn't matter very much at all for marketing.

I once reviewed research on online buzz for certain popular soda brands. One brand hadn't invested much in online marketing and had done very little with social media at that point, but there was a fair amount of buzz about its products from people discussing them organically. The other brand had innovated constantly using social media, and there was a lot of buzz about this brand, but almost all the buzz was about its marketing, while buzz about its products was minimal.

I always turn back to that research when I get so excited about big, bold, innovative ideas. As important as I think I am as a marketing blogger, most brands would fail miserably if they only reached the echo chamber of my peers among bloggers and advertising trade publications. Perhaps, in the example above, marketing pundits did drink more of the second brand's soda, but there are maybe a couple hundred thousand people reading marketing trades compared to the couple hundred million that the brand really was trying to reach.

It's execution that matters, in a way that achieves a marketer's business objectives. It's hard to do something totally new with the cornerstones of social media — namely blogs, social networks, wikis, photo and video sharing, micro-blogging, social bookmarking, and the like. More importantly, marketers don't need to do something ground breaking. What will really break through for them is reaching the audience they want to reach, or harnessing intelligence they can draw actionable insights from, or improving communication with their key constituents. Even if it doesn't get marketing bloggers buzzing, that will still be the innovation they need.

MARKETERSSTUDIO.com

Many Routes to Point B

Len Kendall

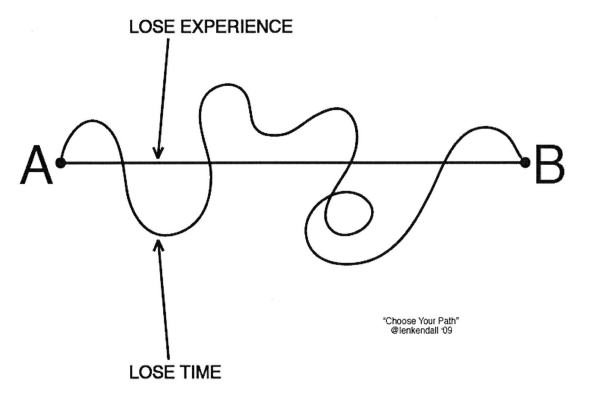

LOSE EXPERIENCE

A   B

LOSE TIME

"Choose Your Path"
@lenkendall '09

Innovation can come in many forms, but I like to categorize them into two basic groups — scheduled or ongoing. A company like Apple goes through a relatively scheduled process of innovation. They take small steps every year to improve their products and generally those innovations are embraced by their fans. A company like Google doesn't have such regimented product releases, and introduces new products when they are ready and invests resources into directions that may never result in a profit. But overall, they come out on top.

As you can see in the illustration above, both paths take you from point A to point B and they can both do so successfully. A person or organization simply needs to choose which path is ideal for them.

In my own case, I enjoy the direct path. It allows me to go through a short process and reach an outcome that I can quickly start optimizing for the best outcome. It also lets me start working on "innovating" other new projects without having the bulk of the previous clouding my mind. But again, this is not the optimal path for all. I do miss the chances to stumble across relevant discoveries and creative options (or at least more of them).

So looking at the image above, how do you choose what works for you and the projects you're working on?

Do you want to lose time or do you want to lose experience?

CONSTRUCTIVEGRUMPINESS.com

Innovation and Execution

Brett Macfarlane

The funny thing about innovation is ideas are bountiful and never before have there been so many great ideas. In addition to creative professionals relentlessly developing ideas now, anyone can go from bitching about something over a coffee to formally cataloging an idea online and essentially submitting it for consideration through fan pages, suggestion boxes or the increasing social-ness of all mediums. Even if only 1–2 percent of all ideas are truly great the absolute number of great ideas is surely increasing.

However, if there is a glut of great ideas why are there still so many mediocre, unoriginal or marginally improved products going to market? Simple, humans get in the way. No matter how much movies, TV shows and even ads themselves mock blunt tools like focus groups, our over reliance on them continues to water down greatness.

Input and feedback is important but shouldn't we try using social tools to get closer to end users in cleaner contexts with less baggage to get better quality feedback? Then again, is that really a better way or just a different way of doing the same thing? Just another way to analyze "innovations" that aren't really that innovative?

Tragically, much of the initial applications of new social tools was to recreate existing ideas more quickly, cheaply or simply leveraging the novelty of anyone being able to make a 30 second TV spot. The greater pursuit or question of our time is whether we can generate an entirely new breed of ideas or execute ideas that were previously impossible to do so. What if we look at social tools as a way to develop or make ideas completely different from anything we've ever know?

There are many well-trodden processes for innovation from the rigid to complete chaos. They can all work, but completely different outcomes require completely different processes. As brand's touch points and media plans fragment beyond points of manageability maybe principals like crowd sourcing and social collaboration are the only way to simply develop complex ideas or to take them to market.

Reality is, although we live at a time where creating, propagating and discovering a great idea holds increasingly negligible barriers we still live in a world of finite time, budgets and resources. We're pretty good at creating the types of innovations we're familiar with, but to create something unconventional we need some develop unconventional processes.

BRETTMACFARLANE.TYPEPAD.com

120

Give People Something Worth Talking About

Frank Striefler

INNOVATION

BRAND

EXPERIENCES   CONVERSATION

Create better realities, not just better images. In today's hyper-connected society, social media is extinguishing mediocrity faster than ever, making the age-old mantra of the analog days, "innovate or die," even more critical. In a conversation-driven world, it's more important what people say about your brand than what brands say about themselves. Consumers talk about what brands are *doing* for them, not what brands are *saying* to them. So give people something to talk about and use innovation to create super-satisfying experiences that people actually like to talk about. Since reality will always trump image, marketers need to start creating real value vs only perceived value.

Think 365 vs 360. It's time to shift from campaign thinking to conversation thinking. We can no longer take a lazy, matching luggage approach to integration, with a few major campaigns per year. Being "always on" means moving from singular, rotating messaging toward multiple, coherent streams of ideas. This means shifting from simplistic, one-dimensional, reduced executions to complex, multidimensional, rich executions. It challenges us to move from highly polished big campaigns to a coordinated, continuous array of strategic strikes in order to be more in sync with culture and to stay ahead of competitors. As with people, a brand is a sum of its experiences — a brand built on many coherent ideas is more interesting than a brand built on fewer consistent messages.

Build long-term platforms. Brands can't go dark anymore. Brands must build long term platforms as permanent brand destinations and an indispensable part of people's daily lives. Branded platforms build their audience and value increasingly over time by providing continued utility and/or entertainment. Conversation thinking does not necessarily mean abandoning campaigns altogether. It means using campaigns to invite new participation, kick off new conversations, and amplify and expand the existing conversations.

Start with a social idea, not social platforms. When it comes to employing a social media strategy, too often it starts with social media platforms focusing on tools and technologies. Start instead with ideas that have social currency and support the brand's role in culture and/or its social mission. Do something people care about and make sure it's something that you personally would want share with your friends in the real world. Having the tools to share stories doesn't mean we don't need to earn the right to be shared P2P any less.

LINKEDIN.com/in/striefler

Having an Idea Isn't Enough

Corentin Monot

The internet is full of abandoned villages, sites or places vaguely interesting at some point that have lost their edge and where nobody is coming back anymore. The statistics are quite interesting — 60 percent of Twitter users stop using it after only one month for instance (source: Nicholas Carlson).

What does it tells us? The first thing is that only people with real passion and knowledge about a specific subject will make the effort to create and nurture conversations over time. However, the most important thing relies on the fact that most projects fail because people believe solely in the power of an idea.

I feel weird about writing that an idea isn't the most important thing because I keep telling my clients that they shouldn't jump on a piece of technology before they actually have an idea or a problem to solve.

Obviously, I am not saying that an idea isn't important, but just coming up with one isn't enough. If you want your project to be successful you have to think like an entrepreneur.

Most people don't give legs to the ideas. This, to my knowledge, is the main reason why social media projects are failing. Too many people think social media projects are a fast and cost-effective way to communicate when in fact they should think about them as products or services. The difference is that you need money to promote your product/service beyond the ineffective seeding campaigns.

To give you a concrete example, I worked on a project for Nissan UK called "100% Urban Guide" (see urban-guide.co.uk). The aim was to bring the QASHQAI positioning, "100% Urban Proof," to life. We decided to create a grassroots guide for the main UK cities by aggregating content people wrote organically on various disconnected parts of the internet. The project was very well received when we launched it, but we didn't give the idea enough legs and spent most of the budget on the build of the platform itself. An idea like this one could easily become the future of the brand proposition across all media; however, in order to do so, the idea must be promoted in the first place and not be used to support an above-the-line campaign.

Next time you come up with a social media idea you will know you've done half of the job — now give some legs to this idea!

ORGANIC-FROG.com

Social Media — A Curmudgeon's View

Ernie Mosteller
ıııııııııııııııııııııııııııııııııııııı

I'm not a complete curmudgeon when it comes to all things social media, though I can get cranky. Clearly, I've embraced social media for a long time. Why else would I be writing here? My personal harrumph isn't about social media (the space) so much as it is about social media (the silver marketing bullet.)

Yes, social media has changed the conversation. It's flipped on its head the ways brands and customers interact. But if the space itself teaches us anything, it should teach us that there is no single formula-driven solution to effective conversation and relationship building. After all, social media isn't a thing. It's a lot of things. It might not even truly be defined as a space anymore. It could be, in essence, a method and protocol for conversation. But it's definitely not a silver bullet.

The truth is, there can only be one silver bullet for marketing, and that job was taken long ago —a great product is your bullet. Nothing else will ever supplant it. Marketing tactics can only enhance it. As marketing tactics go, social media represents quite a few really good ones. Just, not the only ones.

Hype around social media positions the space as the purer way for brands and customers to interact. A two way street that changes the traditional dynamic, and favors both the customer and the smart brand that plays smartly in that street. It lauds social media as a game-changer that has shifted consumer behavior and attitudes online and off. And it warns the marketer that no significant contemporary marketing effort is complete without some significant effort in social media. In fact, all of the above hype isn't hype. It's truth.

But ...

But the other truth is (and let's keep with the bullet analogy here) ground troops are more effective with air cover. And air campaigns aren't complete without a ground game. For a significant brand to carve out a significant place in the general culture, a holistic view of communications — including social, web, and traditional — wins hearts, minds and the battle.

The voice of traditional is now informed by social. That's both true, and a significant shift. But let's not forget that social can itself be fueled by the catalyst of traditional support. When they work hand in hand, each works best. When they work together for a great product, nothing works better.

ıı
ERNIEMOSTELLER.com

Innovation Is "Overrated"

Christopher Morris

In the white space of my life (not online), I'm an avid reader of books. Recently, I found a gem at a used book store, *The Internet for Dummies* (2nd ed), published way back in 1994. Most people would find this to be an out-of-date internet reference guide (and it is), but actually it's an interesting window into the world of early online computing. Aside from email, it seems that finding information on the internet involved navigating cumbersome and complicated menus (through programs such as Gopher) or subscribing to a Usenet newsgroup and filtering messages.

But along came Mosaic, the first popular web browser (eventually evolving into Netscape), which changed the world with its intuitive point-and-click interface.

Mosaic was just beginning to make ripples when the *Internet for Dummies* book I mentioned was being put together. It warrants a whopping four pages out of over four hundred. Here are the author's short-sighted words underneath the heading "So What About Mosaic?" in the book: "You have doubtless heard all about Mosaic, the 'killer application of the internet.' So why haven't we discussed it yet? Well, it's somewhat overrated, but it's still pretty cool, so here it is."

What a begrudging endorsement! An invention that Thomas Friedman attributes as one of ten "forces that flattened the world" in his book *The World is Flat* is deemed "overrated" at the time.

Let's also look at Pixar Films, making waves around the same time as Mosaic with its first feature film *Toy Story*. Founder John Lasseter originally worked at Disney. In the 1980s he was fired after trying to convince the studio to use computer animation in its films to add depth and dimension (overrated?). If you've ever watched any Pixar movies, you know the end of that story — almost every animated feature film today is done using computer animation.

But, to the *Internet for Dummies'* author's credit, much of new technology *is* overrated — Segway or Second Life anyone?

Thus, before getting busy with social media (or emerging technologies), ask questions such as "is it something that makes a service or product easier or better for customers? Is there real value in this new application? How does it align with our mission?"

It comes down to:

- Is there a demand? (think Mosaic.)
- Or will your new innovative idea *create* demand? (think Pixar.)

SUBLIMEGOODNESS.com

Innovation Is More Than a Buzzword

Tamera Kremer

As social media matures, it provides a unique opportunity for companies to take their business to the next level and instill a culture of innovation and collaboration across the enterprise. At this point in history, brands can no longer afford to think in silos and talk at customers. The landscape has changed and the old method of "interaction" (push messaging) doesn't work. People are conversing every day online, and to let you into their networks and social circle you must provide value and be a real human being, not a faceless brand. No one wants to speak to a corporate robot.

Real, honest feedback is not something to be feared, but embraced. Learning from people who are passionate about your company, or critical of it, provides an unparalleled opportunity to evolve and become better at what you do. Tapping into the collective takes time and a willingness to transform, but can reap benefits that you may not anticipate, including increased trust, research and development you didn't actively seek out, and ideas you hadn't thought of but make perfect business sense.

Crowdsourcing is the hot term, but the benefits are only truly realized when you are at the table participating, listening, and learning. Instead of trying to force-fit your product or message into an expensive ad that you hope people will pay attention to, passionate people will let you know what it is about your brand they care about and are willing to share with their friends and neighbors, and what they won't. The social web is a realtime focus group; one you aren't "in control of," but are "a part of."

In order to be "a part of" this realtime world, you will need to empower your employees to participate in social channels. While for some this will seem to be a suck on productivity, the reverse is actually the case. You can foster a more collaborative and innovative work environment that allows people to bring forward ideas and solutions for the benefit of the business as a whole. Sure, some people will abuse that trust, but that's a hiring problem, not a social media problem.

To be truly innovative you need to believe in evolving your business. And the one thing about evolution is that it isn't static.

31.WILDFIRESTRATEGY.com

Shake Up and Stir

Cathryn Hrudicka

We always ask, "What's next?" — especially when it comes to the internet and social media. Rather than focus on the tools, I think it's more essential to focus first on people.

As social media and social networks have become widely adopted by corporations, nonprofits, small businesses and individuals, an amazing shake-up is taking place in our organizations and the ways we work. The fact that using these tools requires transparency and openness means that social users are thinking more creatively and driving innovation, both inside and outside of their organizations.

We can expect to see a constant spiral of workplace innovation driving the creation of new social tools and uses, and vice-versa.

How can we use social media, social networks and online communities more creatively to drive and sustain innovation?

Here are some questions to ask when strategizing and planning a social media project:

- At the beginning of each specific project, are we thoroughly surveying the audience or customers, rather than simply assuming that Twitter, Facebook, LinkedIn and a blog are the way to go? Are we matching online strategy and tools to where each specific audience is on the web?

- Is there a plan for creating compelling content, including video, audio and images, to tell a story and interact, using a variety of media?

- In our workplaces, are we openly sharing ideas and developing online platforms to bridge the gap between good ideas and finding co-workers and advocates who can help us develop ideas, collaborate, and acquire resources to bring them to fruition?

- Are we approaching the creation of a social media team as we would organize an innovation team, including diverse personalities, thinkers and doers who take different creative roles, as they would in another type of innovation project?

- Are we choosing a social media team of collaborators who can work effectively together, question and support each other?

- Are we integrating social media across departments so it's not "stuck in PR or marketing," when it should be an integral part of every department?

- Are we thinking creatively about how to organize, use and evaluate internal and external social media and communities?

- Are we developing new metrics—meaningful methods of measuring results?

- Are we shaking up the status quo?

- Is it working?

New Media, Same Difference

Mark McGuinness

Everything in this world is a two-edged sword.
Chiselled stone tablets — durable but labor-intensive.
Illuminated manuscripts in Latin — beautiful but only for the few.
Printing presses — democratised learning but led to a new class of gatekeeper.
Now social media gives us all our own printing presses.

There has never been such a wealth of new creations — and never such a volume of crap.
There have never been so many opportunities for creators — and never so many competitors.
There have never been so many sources of inspiration — and never so many distractions.

As always, the ones who succeed will be the ones who resolve this creative tension.
The ones making remarkable things, not churning out "content."
The ones busy collaborating, not competing.
The ones who are inspired and focused, not distracted.

Right now, we're entranced by the tools. But soon, we'll take them for granted.
They'll become invisible — just like the chisel, the quill, the printing press, the typewriter.
At that point, it won't be enough to know about the tools.
As always, it will come down to what you are offering, to whom, and why it matters.

LATERALACTION.com

Innovation: How Do You Get There?

Duane Brown

Innovation is about going somewhere and not knowing how you are going to get there. Evolution is about building on something and knowing how you are going to get there. Not knowing how you're going to get there is the key difference between innovation and evolution. To be a true innovator you need to have three traits (in my opinion):

Passion

Having a passion for what you do is important in life. However, having passion is more important when you want to innovate. That passion is going to drive you and keep your skin in the game when many people will have left the game all together. When you are passionate about life and work … it never feels like work.

Risk Taker

Nothing has ever been achieved in this world by being a follower. Leaders innovative and show people new possibilities and options that never occurred to them before. If you are going to seriously innovate, then you are going to need to take a huge amount of risk and get outside of your comfort zone. Only then can you take your passion with your ability to take risk and show the world what you came up with.

Naïve

We often don't know what we don't know in the world. Being naïve means you just won't believe that there is only one or two or fives ways to publish a book, use Twitter or what you can do with Wordpress. You are only limited by your imagination, which won't be clouded by everything that has come before you with what you are trying to innovate on. Being naïve means you'll experiment and try out new ideas.

When you take some passion, add a mix of risk and throw in naivety, you've just the right combination to innovate in any aspect of your life. This is going to lead you to execute on your new innovation.

Execution

I don't think there is a right or wrong way to execute on innovation. Each situation is unique because each innovation is unique to the industry and world. The only thing that stays constant is the ability for some people to see beyond the forest through the trees and see what's possible when some people only see what's constant. Innovation changes the world and makes you a leader.

CREATIVETRACTION.com

How to "Grow" an Innovation

Oleksandr Skorokhod

The evolution and development of our civilization is tightly connected with innovation. It relates to business, art, science and many other areas of human activity. But how is innovation born? Can we make innovation? And if so, how? These are the most intriguing questions. I want to share three key factors necessary for growing innovation.

Field: Preparation of Appropriate State

Innovations, firstly, are "born" in an innovator's mind as ideas. These ideas are like seeds, needing appropriate conditions for their realization. The most important factor is the state of the innovator's mind — it is the place where it all starts. It is in the "beginner's mind" in the Zen tradition or the "open," "fresh" mind more familiar to Western where the small seeds of future innovations emerge — however unusual or strange they appear at first glance.

So, to start grow an innovation — prepare your mind for new ideas, stay open-minded.

Cultivation: Finding an Appropriate Way

Not all seeds grow due to the lack of some necessary conditions. Not all ideas can be realized due to technical, financial, political or other factors. So the innovator needs to find a way to make an idea a reality. It takes time, during which a selection of ideas take place. It also needs patience. Never stop half-way. Remember that Edison had about 10,000 attempts before he succeeded in making an electric lamp.

Be ready to keep searching for the way how to make your innovation a reality.

Market: Realization — Bringing Your Innovation to Market

We could grow excellent oranges or apples in our garden, but if we don't share it with people, then they won't have an opportunity to appreciate their true value. Such situations are similar with innovations. Only when an innovation comes from the laboratory to market, can it become useful in our day-to-day life.

Finally, please bring your innovation to as many people as you can in order to make their lives easier and more comfortable.

So, from this moment you know the three factors necessary to grow innovation. You can use them. You should use them. Please, find an opportunity to make innovations in any area you would like to and make people's lives happier.

H.ua/profile/58299

No Risk, No Reward

Dustin Jacobsen

You don't have to look far to know the world is changing at an ever-increasing pace. Technology helps to facilitate some of the change, but is only part of the equation. Although technology companies tend to be the ones getting the most attention with their thousand percent growth charts and press releases with millions of dollars of investment capital changing hands, it's the population as a whole that's the force behind change.

There isn't a one-size-fits-all approach for innovation, especially for emerging technologies. The closer you get to the cutting edge the more likely it is that the technology or service won't be around a year from now.

Failure needs to be OK. While launching the next big campaign is important, the process of engaging consumers and learning from the experience is important.

Innovation is a long term investment. Be patient. There are a few organizations with innovation built into the DNA of the organization — but this is the exception. Even the definition of "innovative" varies from one organization to the next.

Have a plan. Don't expect to just stumble upon the next big idea. Innovation takes resources, time and a lot of trial and error. While innovation doesn't have to be expensive, be realistic about the amount of time, energy, dedication and persistence it will take.

Start small and capitalize on your wins. Don't expect to see a huge win right out of the gate. If you start with a small project with reasonable goals and gain the confidence of your peers, they're more likely to support you in your on-going endeavors. You can't go from zero to 100 without a huge amount of risk. Take calculated risks and learn along the way.

Closely monitor trends. Who are your customers? Where do they spend their time? What customer needs can be addressed? How is the culture changing? Addressing an existing need is a shortcut to the finish line.

Continuously refine and improve. One of the many challenges of being innovative is the reality that many projects will fail. In some cases a failure will be defined as getting beat to market by a competitor or startup. In other cases, it may be less adoption of the product than expected. Or maybe just too expensive. This is where continuous improvement comes into play. With realistic expectations, you'll know a winner when you see it.

SHAKEGENTLY.com

Social Media — Simply Tactics, Not the Objective

Paul Williams

Marketing teams are scrambling — trying to make sure they stay part of the "conversation" armed with the latest social media magic marketing bullets.

Too often, hype causes us to make impulsive decisions regarding our tactics. We forget social media is one kind of "how" — just a fraction of the full range of tools available to marketers and business owners.

To ensure the right tactics, have your objectives in mind and understand your target customers. Knowing the Who, Why, What, When, and Where will lead you to the appropriate How.

Who? Specifics about your target customer(s). What gender and groups do you target? What are the demographics of this potential or existing customer?

Why? What is the relevant reason to reach this customer? What call to action should take place? Trial? Visit? Purchase? Frequency? To spread word of mouth?

What? What is the focus? A product, a service, an event?

When? What is the occasion they need/want your product or service? When do they need you most? An aspirin brand responds to "I have a headache, I need pain relief." Understanding the "when" also helps develop the relevant language of your communication.

Where? Where are your customers when they're receptive to your message? At home, in transit, at work, while shopping, on the computer, while relaxing, at your location?

How? The tools to effectively reach someone. Media, social or otherwise… anything from a print ad, Twitter, or skywriting.

Start with your established business objective, your goal. Then, move through the question and answer chain to determine your appropriate tactic(s) and:

- Reach your **Who** (specific customers)
- Using the appropriate **How** (vehicle)
- In the right **Where** (location)
- Addressing the right **When** (need)
- With the appropriate and specific **What** (product/service/event), and
- With the right **Why** (reason).

Of course, don't forget to assess if the tactic is appropriate for your brand, if you have the time and money to support it, and, if it can be logistically implemented.

In this Age of Conversation you are smart to revisit your marketing plan on a regular basis and make sure you are using the best tools. However, next time someone suggests implementing the latest marketing trend, first make sure it is the right answer to your questions.

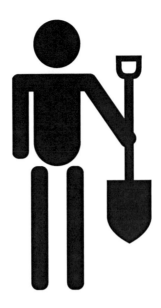

Influence

The Influence of Not Being Influenced

Amy Jussel

"This blog can't be bought" was an icon I considered using amidst the new media kerfluffle about embedded branding and bloggers for hire, because to me, being raw and real, with service-driven, meaningful content adds value to a conversation that "pays off" in trust and return on influence (ROI) far beyond analytics of "digerati bigwigs" and tracking numbers, clicks and followers.

With an increasingly exhausted public struggling to sift "what's real" in everything from reality shows to product placement (savvy consumers know buzz can be bought, viral can be "seeded" and vested interests can permeate citizen journalism as well as mainstream media) the open ended question we're all trying to grapple with is, "How do you monetize influence in a trust-based economy?"

I won't use the hackneyed "a" word (authenticity) or even "b" words (brand-building) even though both are essential in earning trust via reputation. I'm going to hang my hat on the "c" words of creating credibility through content while curating a conversation that adds value to the readers without the perception of asking for something in return.

I say perception, because in this time-pinched world we're asking for the most coveted asset of all, even a nanosecond of influence or attention.

Influence is not a commodity to be brokered, but rather an intimacy to be earned. Those who "speed date" based on appearance and numbers alone will no doubt miss the nuanced complexity of a longer term, interpersonal relationship driven by collaboration and genuine compatibility. Same goes for marketing partners, affiliates, and sponsors for that matter.

If you're using social media to recruit copious quantities of "sheeple" that flock to a herd without quite knowing why, that's not "influence." Rather than a "pop up quickly, fizzle out fast," it takes perseverance finding and befriending fellow thought leaders who recognize, respect, and evangelize your vision with integrity.

I dare say if we'd chosen to "jump start" our nonprofit's financial solvency by taking traditional funding paths or accepting "any ol' donor check" instead of remaining unencumbered *sans* conflict of interest throughout our "perpetual beta" phase ... we wouldn't have the "currency of credibility" to propel us to the next phase of sustainability with deeper, more meaningful and *lasting* conversations we're having now.

Social media is the open invitation — "know me, know my brand."

Influence will sort itself out from there.

SHAPINGYOUTH.org

Influence — A Song of Passion and Proximity

Katie Chatfield

You might have heard of targeting "influencers" as a new term for ultra-targeted word of mouth strategy in the social media space. I've heard "how much is an influencer worth?" and "how many followers does an influencer have?" and my favorite, "How much should I pay an influencer to plug my product?"

Influence is not another term for reach. It's not a media measurement. It is not a placement strategy.

There are people who have influence … and people who might influence other's opinion about you.

You'll want to gather the latter for your client or your brand. That should be your goal — a growing collection of the right people telling brand building, retail driving stories. I call these people "resonant agents." Resonant because they amplify the brand system's energy, and create bigger waves than other people. Agents because they're willing to take on tasks and they're willing to act on your account.

And the former? Who is the influencer?

That would be you.

You need to influence the resonant agent. Try to understand what resonance is for your brand and its context; try to find out who the most resonating agents are in that system.

Try to find the people that count, rather than just counting the people because ultimately, creating ideas that influence really isn't about what gets served, but about what serves your brand and the people who care about it.

Mack Collier, in his presentation "What Rock stars Can Teach You About Kicking Ass With Social Media," and with his tweet "Social Media needs fewer Rock stars, and more rockstar ideas," talks about using reach and marketing for good.

And I agree … but "rock star" ideas really only work *if you actually are a rock star*. You can't build an audience and grow fans if you don't deliver great experiences. You don't get gigs or airplay or t-shirt sales without the songs, the swagger and the talent.

You've got to write them. And they've got to be good. You've got to earn it.

So earn it. Be a rock star. Create amazing experiences. Hold 150,000 people in the palm of your hand. Have 8 million people streaming and breathless with your every move.

Do epic shit. Then listen.

The ones in the front row singing along are the future captains of your fan clubs, your resonant agents. Create the right ideas to influence them and you can create beautiful music together.

KATIECHATFIELD.WORDPRESS.com

Influence

Mark Earls

The bad news: we have got influence upside-down.

It's not something people exert on each other, but something they accept from each other; it's a pull — not a push thing.

We worry about the *influencers* when the *influenced* should be our concern; about recommendation and advocacy when *eyeline* — how easy it is to see someone else's adoption of a particular idea or behaviour or their excitement or anger — is what should be concerning us.

To be blunt, it seems like we're squeezing old persuasion thinking from the TV age into human and social clothes: persuasive propositions distributed by high-rating and highly trusted individuals to beat up on the dumb punters.

The good news: you can always turn it rightside up!

P.S. Don't feel bad if you also fall into this McLuhanite trap: most everyone around here has also got a vertical hold problem!

HERD.TYPEPAD.com

137

The Importance of Influence: How Influence Increases Income

Tinu Abayomi-Paul

One of the reasons influence is so important is because it can't be bought.

Sure, if you had the budget, you could spend millions of dollars on advertising, and run an advertising campaign that could reach into the home of everyone with a TV set, a computer, or a cell phone. But once you reached everyone, then what?

You can't force people to buy, but you can influence them.

At some point you'll have to rely on your ability to get your audience to take the action you most desire. That means influence is important to everyone. Which brings us back to our point — learning to wield influence is important is partly because it can only be earned, not bought.

But is influence available to everyone?

For centuries, not only did you need to work, be schooled, or socialize with people of wealth and status to have a chance at becoming influential, you had to do so at an adjacent level of status to even be considered. There was a time, as recently as the 1990s, where the path to wealth and status and the path to influence were identical. You couldn't become influential without being both wealthy and of some social status. One certainly couldn't become wealthy or achieve status through influence.

But the world has changed dramatically in the past few decades. Few people even see this change for the jaw-dropping revelation it is — influence is itself a currency.

If you can learn how to consistently influence a certain percentage of people in a group to take a desired action, you can even trade on that skill as a source of income.

To you, that means you need to do three things to use your influence to make more money:

1. Consistently communicate with as much of your niche market as you can
2. Become the default voice of expertise and authority
3. Increase the number of people who take an action that will increase your income at every contact.

If you are influential, those three steps will make all your communications with your audience more profitable, whether through a new value exchange with existing customers, or expanding your audience to include new prospects.

Of course, the active ingredient in this recipe is influence. It's not as simple to learn how to become more influential, but there are some great resources in this book to help you on your way.

ASKTINU.com

The Heart of Influence

Trey Pennington

Those who get and have influence through social media are those who give. Influence is not about collecting followers or friends (or even the number of downloads, embeds or favorites). Instead, it's about giving attention, connections, content, and assistance around three human dynamics:

1. Everyone wants to be heard

2. Everyone wants to be understood

3. Everyone wants to know his or her life matters

The degree to which you give away the resources you have to address these dynamics — to facilitate your neighbor's quest for significance — is the degree to which you'll enjoy influence through social media.

If you're a small business owner, use social media to give your customers a voice in your business. Use polls, questionnaires, and surveys to ask questions about things that matter to them. Resist the urge to use social media to distribute junk mail (like discount offers).

If you're a political leader (or wannabe), use social media to bring people together in the offline world to voice their hopes, dreams, fears, concerns, and ideas. When you do, you'll also create a platform for them to hear the same from their neighbors. Use social media to draw together; give your presence with them to build them together. Resist the urge to use social media to do the devil's work of "getting our message out."

As you're using social media to give a voice to your customers and bring people together, you'll be addressing dynamics one and two: to be heard, to be understood. You'll also be learning about what matters to them. You'll be experiencing the remarkable new opportunity afforded through social media — two way and multi-way communication between passionate people. While you're doing the listening and seeking to understand, you'll gain insight into the necessary elements, the missing elements, of their quests for significance. With that insight, you'll be in position to facilitate their pursuit of meaning.

When you use social media give away what you have to listen, to understand, and to facilitate your neighbors' quests for significance, you'll be a welcome influence in their lives. Don't look at social media as an easy way for you to get what you want; see it as a way to give others what they need. Remember the time-tested admonition of Zig Ziglar, "You can have everything in life you want, if you'll just help enough people get what they want."

TREYPENNINGTON.com

The New Symbiosis of Professional Networks: A Research Study on the Impact of Social Media on Professional Decision-making

Vanessa DiMauro

Everyone is asserting that social media is the new form of relationship marketing. However, little is known about the impact of social media to change behaviors, or the potential to alter professional's decision-making processes. While most are trying to capture the buyer's mindshare, few understand what, success looks like, and in many cases, are actually missing what decision-makers really want.

To fill this gap, Don Bulmer, SAP and I conducted a research study, "The New Symbiosis of Professional Networks," to examine the role social media has on decision-making among enterprise users (see www. newsymbiosis.com). In the summer of 2009, we surveyed 356 participants on how they use online communities and professional networks to inform their professional decisions. Twenty-three percent of survey takers were CEOs. All respondents were either the decision-makers or influenced the decision process. Company size ranged from less than 100 to over 50,000 full-time employees, Age was well distributed, and 25 countries were represented, with 58 percent of respondents living in the US.

Here are the highlights:

Professional decision-making is becoming more social. Traditional influence cycles are disrupted by social media as decision-makers utilize social networks to inform and validate decisions. Professionals want to be collaborative online but do not want to be marketed or sold to online. Ironically, using social media for marketing is reported to be a preferred activity by companies. This is clearly a strategic mismatch that needs to be corrected!

Professionals trust online information almost as much as information gotten from in-person. Information obtained from offline networks still have highest levels of trust with slight advantage over online (offline: 92 percent combined strongly/somewhat trust; online: 83 percent combined strongly/ somewhat trust).

The big three have emerged as leading professional networks: LinkedIn, Facebook and Twitter. The big players in social media are now being used by professionals for decision-making support. The average professional belongs to 3–5 online networks for business use, and LinkedIn, Facebook and Twitter are among the top.

Social Media Peer Groups (SMPG). These have changed the way we do business. Professionals (customers, partners, prospects and employees) utilize social media as a platform for discussion of their ideas, experiences and knowledge.

LEADERNETWORKS.com

Influence: The New 30-Second Spot?

Tim Tyler
⠀⠀⠀⠀⠀⠀⠀⠀⠀⠀

It is time we marketers got busy with social media and serious about selling for our organizations. But how?

Two best-sellers offer a roadmap for how we should harness social influence: *The Influentials* and *The Tipping Point*. Both suggest we should identify the small number of really influential people in our target market, make them advocates and turn them loose to spread the word. All while exploiting the social internet as the magnifier of influence.

Infect sneezers and send them to parties.

Not that different to finding the show with the highest ratings and placing your ad there, really.

But there is now clear evidence that this influence "channel" has all of the subtlety of its medium; people. For example, we now know (see strikeachord.com.au for references):

- Influence does impact sales, it can be measured, but only if the product is "serious/important" (from pharmaceutical research). Serious products encourage consultation, allowing influence and commodity. The product still matters.
- Influence is routinely overrated — people who claim influence in screening surveys often have little. Much better to ask peers to identify the people of real influence in their social network.
- "Influencers" do exist in online networks, but they do not *begin* the propagation of trends. "Susceptibles" do that; influencers join in after theme propagation starts. Duncan Watts found this in his computer models, it has now been confirmed in online forums. To start a trend, the existence of a group of people ready to be influenced is more important than influencers.
- Opinion leaders (those with influence) generate sales when the marketing challenge is persuasion and you already have good levels of product awareness.
- Opinion leaders talking to their social circle do not get you incremental contagion, you get those customers anyway by the nature of social networks and influence
- If you are looking for *incremental* sales through influence, better to identify less loyal customers and encourage them to discuss you with acquaintances — apply the "strength of weak ties."

Getting busy =
Ask people to point out opinion leaders/influencers, not rate themselves.

Determine if the marketing challenge is:

- **Persuasion** — focus on your brand advocates as influencers.
- **Awareness** — you need a larger number of less loyal fans talking widely.

⠀⠀⠀⠀⠀⠀⠀⠀⠀⠀⠀⠀⠀⠀⠀⠀⠀⠀⠀⠀
STRIKEACHORD.com.au

I've Got a LOT of Influence... And So Can You!

Phil Gerbyshak

Influence — it's persuasion and more.

Influence — it's the currency of social media.

Influence — you're either born with it...or you build it.

Influence matters ... a *lot*!

I've got a lot of influence.

Influence means I can send a message into the interwebs, using Twitter, Facebook, LinkedIn, blogs, podcasts, and every other service known to man. If it's good — no, if it's great — and if it's easy for others to share, if it has meaning to enough people, and if it's authentic and worthwhile, it just might take hold like a white dandelion and fly here and there, and pollinate enough of the world to cover a hundred thousand acres of grass in a golden yellow.

And if it's not, it'll hang there, like dew on a blade of grass on a spring morning, just waiting to be spilt onto the ground.

Influence matters ... a *lot*!

And so can you.

Start by showing up ... a *lot*!

Listen to others who already have influence. Watch what they do. See what they see.

Prep the soil by sharing other people's seeds, other remarkable messages.

Water the soil by adding to the other messages.

Leave a comment, your thoughts — always positive, collaborating.

Once the soil is fertile, start spreading your message far and wide.

Write articles.

Send a tweet.

Facebook it.

Invite people into your community, and invite them to help you make the message even better, even more remarkable, even more relevant.

You can't buy influence, you can't rent influence, you can't force your message to *be* influential.

You can build influence ... over time ... slowly at first, and then faster ... a little faster.

And you can lose your influence all at once.

I've got a lot of influence... and so can you!

Don't blow it!

PHILGERBYSHAK.com

How Social Media Can Influence the Structure of Business

Steve Woodruff

There's a "magnification" effect with social media that is already having quite an effect on how business communications get done. More people can receive messages must faster. Connections can be made more easily. Resources can be found using what is becoming a highly interconnected, global "Help Desk." Collaborations can occur through online platforms. And tribes can be assembled around areas of shared interest and concern — all at lightning speed.

Businesses are already adjusting strategies to incorporate social media — but can the very structure of business — at least some business — undergo a radical restructuring? I think so.

Our typical companies have gathered around named corporations, often in geographical locations. However, skilled and creative people may be able to work far more effectively by creating professional opportunity networks — organic networks of trusted, interconnected professionals (and small companies) who help each other find work, and who team up in various configurations to tackle projects without the need to collect as a formal "corporation."

This is already happening, mostly informally, through sites such as LinkedIn, Twitter, and blogs. However, the time is ripe for greater levels of both *ad hoc* and organized collaborations, where the best of the best can get together in cost-effective ways to tackle high value initiatives with great efficiency. Far more people can work remotely, using their best talents, under this model of organic, trust — and reputation-based collaboration. Expect to see social media change, not only how companies market and communicate, but how they organize. Traditional structures may be in for some radical changes!

STEVEWOODRUFF.com

Influence

S. Neil Vineberg

The social web is an emergent 21st century phenomenon enabled by technology allowing conversation through blogs, podcasts, micro-blogging, and communities like MySpace and Facebook. It began just a few years ago. Hundreds of millions around the globe are now socially engaged. We shared our viewpoints on this in the *Age of Conversation 1* and *2*.

Companies, PR firms, ad agencies and lobbyists are surrounding the social web with cash, seeking to exert influence in existing communities, and create new ones around their own brands, shows, events and causes. Companies are reaching into the web like never before, and shifting promotional budgets from TV, radio and print promotion to online. We are also seeing social media transform the online media business; it's happening almost overnight with companies tapping every tool at their disposal to engage online audiences.

In the 1950s and 60s, corporate advertisers saw the power of TV to influence consumers. Ads for Old Gold cigarettes helped teach parents and children how to smoke. TV shows were created specifically for sponsors until the FCC stepped in to limit the amount of advertising shown during an hour long show.

I applaud companies using the social web for customer engagement, building brand awareness and loyalty. Yet the social web is already under Federal Trade Commission (FTC) scrutiny. I have worked with several mommy bloggers with very high integrity. A few, however, were running pay-for-post operations — printing product reviews in exchange for cash — without revealing payments. That is influence gone awry. Now the FTC has put bloggers on notice with a requirement to disclose payments or promotional consideration related to such reviews.

Who holds the greatest influence in the social web? We do. You and me. Let's continue to support a strong Code of Conduct for the social web that requires companies, publishers and bloggers to act with high integrity, honesty and transparency. Let's call out fake communities built by PR firms and lobbyists that seek to create false perceptions of issues in health care, global warming, women's rights, abortion, GLBT rights and other issues. If we cannot police ourselves, just like the FTC stepped into the blogging business, the government may step in to level the playing field for consumers.

It is an honor to participate in this book and I encourage my esteemed colleagues to continue raising the integrity bar as we advise and engage clients on promoting their brands and building influence in the social web.

VINEBERGCOMMUNICATIONS.WORDPRESS.com

Influence for Introverts: Six Ways For Introverts to Influence More While Talking Less

Don Frederickson

I am an introvert and, unfortunately, live in a world that likes heroes. Nevertheless, I lead and influence without authority or title. I don't covet power in the traditional sense. But I like the tone of quiet power and influence. I wish to be an influential advisor and problem solver. But how does an introvert wield influence contrary to conventional thinking about power and influence?

How do you know you are an introvert? Many simply recognize it. Others take a Meyers-Briggs (MBTI) assessment. My MBTI results labeled me "INTJ." In MBTI speak, the "I" means a tendency to "direct … energy primarily inward toward … inner environment, thoughts, and experiences." The label validated a fear. I wanted to be a person prone to action, a hero who "directs energy … outward toward … people and events."

I got over it. I studied it. I also learned about leadership and influence. I learned that as an introvert, I could change the world. Abraham Lincoln and Dwight Eisenhower did it. In fact, I wish more leaders were introverts. As Jonathon Rauch writes, "If we introverts ran the world, it would no doubt be a calmer, saner, more peaceful sort of place" (see http://bit.ly/6syPym).

Here are six recommendations for introverts who want to quietly influence without leaving their introvert zone. My essential message; leverage your introversion. Use your natural tools to talk less but communicate and influence more.

1. Be friendly. Say "hi" and "bye." Don't forget to smile. People will say "yes" to people they like.
2. You are an expert in silence. Use it. A pause in your words adds powerful punctuation.
3. Look people deeply in the eye. People will nod in agreement.
4. Communicate on paper. The times you go to meetings lacking an agenda? Influence the discussion by outlining your thoughts and distribute the paper as a discussion aid. And because you bring paper, volunteer to record and summarize. As Tom Peters says, whoever "writes the summary … wields great power" (see http://bit.ly/4ZO10A).
5. Follow-up fastidiously. Simply put, do what you say.
6. Show gratitude, say thank you. Go a little out of your way with this simple message.

Influence doesn't have to be loud. Influence can emerge from someone who is not the life of the party. Introverts can leverage their introversion to wield more influence. The result will be a calmer and saner world.

LEADQUIETLY.com

"Letting Go" — The New Influence

Steve Roesler

Right now, you — and your audience — are searching Google for something important. You're hoping that customers are finding you the same way. To make sure, you count the characters of your next tweet, sharing the latest blog entry or eBook on Twitter. More insurance? A quick Facebook update seems like a good idea.

Then, you check the conversation or, hopefully, enter into it to find the buzz surrounding you and your product.

Why?

Because you've learned that what your clients say about you is more important than what you say about you. Their story counts.

Does your product thrill them? Are you useful and fresh or vanilla and boring?

Most importantly: What does your brand *do* for your clients?

The Illusion of Control

We used to create the message we wanted people to hear, put it out there, and call it "marketing." We felt "in control." In a one-way communication vacuum, everything appeared to be just fine. (Actually, we had little or no control over what people thought and how they responded.) We'd bump up the ad budget, win some creative awards, and declare victory.

Social media have turned out to be a gift. Their very nature forces two way conversations on those who may not *like* it but who are smart enough to understand they need to do something differently to be a player.

That "something" is the foundation for the *new influence* — first, observing the conversation; then, involving yourself in it.

For those wanting control, that simple formula requires a change. Involvement leads to relationship, relationship requires vulnerability, and vulnerability means relinquishing control.

Changing is always a choice. I believe there are a lot of pragmatic people whose desire to succeed will lead them to choose new ways to influence. So, here are . . .

Three Ways To Get Started

1. Listen, then respond. Once you do engage, be honest. If people are buzzed about you and your brand, be supportive. If they have issues, own them and offer help.

2. Get comfortable with ambiguity. Conversation can seem disjointed and sometimes intimidating. Your job — respond to it, not control it.

3. Be purposeful. You can get pulled in multiple directions. Having a strong purpose is crucial — it becomes the filter through which you listen and respond. It also defines the nature of your voice and is foundational to the influence that you seek.

Momentum, Fluidity, Direction

James G. Lindberg and Sandra Renshaw

Influence — actions affecting behaviors or opinions of people or institutions.

Influence — to flow in — conjures an image of warm water flowing into a basin, but current usage of "influence" is connected to "persuasion," which carries positive or negative emotional charge.

The root — *flu* — is found in "affluent" (abundance flowing), "confluent" (merging), "effluent" (flowing from), "fluid" (flowing under stress, changing shape), and "fluent" (graceful, flowing). Each conjures an image of active fluidity, motion, direction. Influence, like anything that flows, has power — to erode, nourish, lubricate, purify, pollute. These words are not stagnant. Each implies change.

Family and religion influence the very young. Then follows a lifelong, moderating and steadily-increasing force for change from media (TV, movies, web) and a network that may be self-selected or imposed (peers, schools, sales agents, or advocates).

Influence may be benign and beneficent or controlling, deceptive, and injurious.

Traditional media (few-to-many communication) are controlled by the few, nearly always with intent to affect buying or voting behaviors.

Social media are uniquely influential in ways that traditional media could never be. Social media cannot be bought by the few, are more difficult to censor, are more fluid and responsive. The social media is connection-based and millions are connecting.

Consider peer-to-peer video — an entertainer's racist rant and Howard Dean's concession speech scream; erosion comes to mind. In a medium not owned by the few, positive politics works too. Do we trust unfiltered words and actions of social media more than traditional media's reports with occasional slick revisionism by spin doctors?

Most bloggers have agendas (political, civic, celebrity, educational, or financial), and if a blogger's words and images are perceived as valuable and valid, the site endures.

People who use Twitter keep pace by staying connected at multiple levels to friends, communities, and events. The brief, near simultaneous revelation of information to purposeful people has emergent power and direction. Tweeters collectively build consensus as to trustworthy sources and events.

In traditional media few have voice; in social media many have voice. This collective voice has power and influence rivaling that of traditional media. As trust in the few erodes and trust in the many builds, the balance is tipping. Stay connected to see the outcome. The collection of people trading information in social media has momentum, fluidity, and direction — inherently influential, affecting the behaviors and opinions of people and institutions.

PURPLEWREN.com

Unexpected Influence

Jasmin Tragas

I stepped through the doors of Grossi's Grill in Melbourne trying to find a woman based on her description — and there she sat with a beautiful grin. Irina was only in town for a couple of days on a business trip. We had been introduced to one another through a colleague working in Singapore, and she suggested we meet to learn more about my fundraiser. I had no idea what amazing things would eventuate from this meeting.

At first the conversation was a little awkward, because we didn't know much about one another. But soon we started discussing how women in the Philippines were influencing their communities and how they became empowered through microfinance. I shared how people around the world had started making small donations on my blog, how strangers had tweeted about my fundraiser and why I had chosen to do this as a volunteer with Opportunity International Australia.

Irina's eyes lit up. She told me how she had come into a surprisingly early inheritance through fortunate circumstances. She really wanted to make a difference. This petite and well-spoken businesswoman was suddenly suggesting that she might sponsor an entire $10,000 trust group together with another young businesswoman. Beyond my expectations, they wanted to influence an entire community by funding a two-year program for Filipino women and their families to get out of poverty. And yet we had only just met. I felt like pinching myself!

A couple of months later I was promoting my final fundraising activities online. These two generous women decided to surprise me once more by donating $500 each. Their timing was perfect and I reached my goal of creating a trust group!

None of this could have happened if I hadn't discovered a colleague in the UK through social media at work, who then introduced me to his friend in Singapore, who shared the stories from my blog with her friend.

Irina might not use Twitter or write a blog. But the impact of people around the world joining in creative blog challenges and collaborative e-books over several months told a bigger story and reached the ears of a compassionate woman who was able to make a difference.

BLOG.WONDERWEBBY.com

The Power of Positive Influence

Jeanne Dininni

Influence — a powerful concept with an awesome potential for good when fueled by right motives, ethical intentions, and principled business practices.

Exerting our influence on individuals and markets is easier than ever in our current age of social networking and internet interconnectedness. Yet that's precisely what makes influence such a seriously misused commodity. How can we tap the immense potential of this powerhouse of intentionality without succumbing to the enticements of its more negative manifestations?

The following suggestions can help keep you on track in your efforts to use your Influence fairly, prudently and with real impact.

Determine to use your influence as a force for good. Unfortunately, our world contains far too many influential people, companies, ideas, and products that are powered by ulterior personal, corporate, ideological, and/or financial motives. Tempering — or even totally eclipsing — the common quest for the Almighty Dollar with a healthy touch of altruism and *other*-consciousness is bound to create sounder, more people-friendly business practices. And this will translate to brand loyalty for your company. Recognizing the value of influence in making the world a better place can contribute to your own inner harmony, as well.

Recognize that a positive influence is always mutually beneficial. It's only reasonable to assume that you will consider the core realities of your enterprise first, since the survival of your business depends upon it. Yet, by *also* considering the needs of your market, your prospect, your customer, your supplier, and to some extent even your competitor, you will naturally find that your far-sighted, non-self-centered view reaps greater long term rewards than would a myopic, *me-first* marketing strategy. Determine to exert the sort of influence that sends benefits in both directions, thereby creating a climate of mutual prosperity.

Understand the factors that comprise a healthy influence. Factors such as the following all play a vital role in any desirable Influence we exert on others:

- Positive image (setting an inspiring example)
- Knowledge (demonstrating appropriate expertise)
- Reputation (radiating credibility)
- Responsiveness (maintaining other-focus)
- Ethics (operating by your principles)
- Honesty (admitting your mistakes and weaknesses)

Put the above principles into practice and increase your influence. Work on incorporating the above components into your personal and business strategies, and discover how much greater your Influence can be!

The Paradox of Influence in a Connected World

Paul Hebert

Social media has turned a lot on its head … from marketing to fundraising to Presidential elections. Social media is redefining how we get and transfer information. It's also changing what we mean by influence.

Most of us picture influence as something active. Something pushed *at* us. We think of the motivational speaker on the stage, the politico glad-handing the electorate, or the pitchman with the newest, greatest cleanser. But like all the things social media changed — it changed the definition of influence.

Sure, the idea of influence is the same — someone who is influential says (or tweets, posts, links, digs, etc something and others do something differently with that information. But getting to be influential is less about what you say — and more about what you hear.

Paradoxically, influence in the social media space is more about listening than talking. It's about taking the time to find information, listen to multiple streams of thoughts and opinion. Influence is about asking more questions, not providing more answers.

As you wander the social media landscape and run into those that have influence, you will also find those same people follow an almost incalculable number of input streams. Being influential in today's world is about taking the time to listen and process. Influence is about adding value to the barrage of inputs — not simply regurgitating the same tweet or the same blog posts. Influence is about thinking and adding value.

Getting Influence

Instead of worrying about getting influence worry about getting connected and worry about listening. The first step in influence is following — following others who think, discuss, and analyze. Most people worry about their followers and assume that followers equal influence. But to really have influence you need to be a follower first.

Follow first. Listen to the social network for your niche and think about what is being said. Think about how it impacts you personally — if you're in business, how does that information affect your customers and your targeted customers? How can you add value to that stream?

Simply re-tweeting or following the same people as everyone else is nothing more than being cult-like. True influencers are followers first and influentials second. Don't make the mistake of equating following with influence. It's who you follow that makes you influential not who follows you.

At least at first.

I2I-ALIGN.com

Social Media ROCKS

Timothy L. Johnson

"No! No! No! And, oh, by the way, did I mention, NO? I WON'T BLOG!"

That was my initial reaction to social media when approached by a friend and colleague four years ago. His well-meaning suggestion was intended to help me launch my first book. Eventually, I conceded to "give the darn thing a try" and carpefactum.com was launched.

Fast forward to the present day. My company blog is still going. I am now writing regularly for two other blogs (officepolitics.com and iowabiz.com). I am active on Facebook, LinkedIn, and Twitter.

But what has all of this social media stuff actually *accomplished* for me? In short, social media ROCKS my world:

Relationships — my reach and influence has expanded around the world. I've "met" people from all walks of life who share my vision and philosophy, and I've forged some rich friendships with many people whom I would never have even encountered.

Opportunities — because of my social media presence, I've been invited to speak and consult with audiences around the nation. It's a much wider world out there than the cadre of cubicles surrounding you. As I launch my third book, I'm able to leverage those opportunities for a broader reach as I get others to help me with my marketing.

Credibility — my clients now come to me for advice and input on social media strategy. They want to know how to reach the right audiences effectively. I'm able to leverage my knowledge of human nature and office politics to help them, and they view me as a social media "subject matter expert." Recently, a client who was void of social media strategies asked me to research what was being said about their products; they were surprised (and appreciative) to learn the results.

Karma — I've learned the biggest lesson of social media is in giving. The more you give away, the more you get back from others. The blogosphere is a big place where a lot of really nice people make the positive energy flow.

Symbiosis — social media does not operate in a vacuum. I've learned how to make all of the tools work together with my speaking, writing, and consulting. Together, they propel my brand to new frontiers.

Not all social media experiences are the same for everyone. Test it, play with it, adjust it, and mold it. I'll bet it ROCKS for you, too.

CARPEFACTUM.com

Who Is the Real Social Media Influencer?

Arun Rajagopal

There are many ways to measure influence in social media. The success of a blog can be gauged in terms of number of visitors, blog subscribers, authority/ranking or comments. One's influence on Twitter can be measured by number of followers, retweets generated and presence in lists. On YouTube, the number of channel subscribers, comments and views determine the popularity of your videos. Number of friends, likes and comments show how big a star you are on Facebook. Big kahunas enjoy some of the largest networks on LinkedIn. Give or take any social media channel, there are metrics available to measure your influence in a quantitative fashion.

While these numbers are indicative of the quality or value offered by a social media influencer, there is one metric that is hard to measure, but very easy to identify. The Social Media Goodness Index.

Ever since my involvement with social media began, I have come across a couple of stellar individuals who always strive to deliver quality and value in everything they do. They are the ones who understand the big picture of social media and are tirelessly educating us on how to benefit from it well. They use their social media smarts to make the world around them a richer place. They enrich us with their wit, wisdom and passion to do good. Their online personas are a true reflection of who they are in real life. They operate on principles of trust, transparency and integrity. They are approachable and reach out to you when you need them, across oceans and time zones. They put the needs of a community before them. These are the real social media influencers for me.

These social media stars are hard to place in any ranking or index. However, they stand out in any community. Because true communities are built around them. They form my Social Media Goodness Index.

The good news: many of these real social media influencers are a part of *The Age of Conversation*. Over the years to come, social media will undoubtedly change and take new forms from what we make of it today. However, these leaders will be at the forefront, championing the change and making the social media world a better place for all of us.

ARUNRAJAGOPAL.com

Influencing People in B2B Marketing

David Koopmans

"Social influence occurs when an individual's thoughts or actions are affected by other people."
— Wikipedia

Influencing Irrational People in B2B Marketing

If you're marketing anything, your goal is to infl uence people. If you sell to other businesses (B2B), you also know that your buyers often spend a lot of time evaluating options before they buy, because their most important concern in buying is avoiding risk (see Gord Hotchkiss, *The Buyersphere Project,* BookSurge Publishing, 2009); personal risk (Will this decision get me sacked or promoted?) and corporate risk (Will this put me at an advantage or disadvantage?).

So what does that have to do with influence? When buyers look for advice, they turn to two main sources; their network and the media (and maybe some of your marketing materials). Social media merges their network and media into one — now people in a buyer's network become part of the media and people expand their traditional "real" network exponentially through social media.

The reason people with influence play such an important role is that as buyers, we are not rational. For all the evaluation people undertake before buying your product, most of the time they'll pick a recommendation by someone they *trust,* over the facts and figures from someone they don't.

So What Can You Do?

As a marketer, you're already influencing people, so the question is how you use social media to extend what you are doing now.

Relationships with the people that influence your market have always been a powerful marketing asset. In the old days, they were a handful of journalists, some of your customers and some business partners, most likely in the city you live in.

So who are the people that influence your market? Maybe they are from traditional media (social media is now a great source of ideas for them) or self appointed experts. Focusing your efforts on influencing them rather than the whole market is more manageable, more targeted and therefore more likely to be effective.

Building Trust

Successful influencers in social media have another characteristic —they work hard at building trust and respect in their networks by being transparent about their motivation and by offering quality in their content. It's not the size of someone's network, or the frequency of publishing that makes people influential. Just because some very influential people in social media have large networks and publish frequently, doesn't mean a thing. If you can publish good content to the right audience, you will be influential.

Is it a Good Investment of Your Time?

In B2B marketing, the answer must be "yes." Social media (like all media) helps people evaluate buying options, and if you have influence in your media niche, it will pay. The tools may have changed, but the strategic logic is the same.

MOKUMMARKETING.com/blog

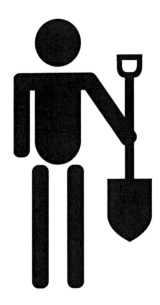

Getting to Work

Outside-in Thinking: Driving Business Success Through Data and Conversation

Beth Harte

Whether you're new to implementing the concept of social media or you work for an organization that's been actively engaged in it for years, you have probably recognized that social media conversations run much deeper than what they appear to be on the surface. Those who believe in the merit of social media as a business process recognize that organizations are no longer in the proverbial driver's seat when it comes to brand relationships. Consumers/customers are determining the course of action (when, where, why, how, etc.) they take with brands.

This fundamental change requires organizations to get to work in changing business processes so that they can better drive business success. One way to do this is by utilizing outside-in thinking and ongoing conversation.

Outside-In Thinking: Gathering Data

Most organizations use inside-out thinking to determine their business processes and marketing. It's what they think the market wants or how they think they should interact with the market. Obviously, outsidein thinking is quite the opposite. It's about understanding and embracing what's truly going on in the market through collected data. Data can take the form of demographics, psychographics, sociographics and ethnographics. Social media and monitoring tools allow organizations to gather quantitative and qualitative data that can show an organization how to take the journey with consumers/customers. Sounds easier said than done, right? Being successful with outside-in thinking requires a complete culture change, which isn't easy; it's hard work.

Outside-In Thinking: Engaging in Conversation

Let's pretend your organization has all of the data it could ever want. Now what? Let's remember that social media puts organizations right in front of their consumers/customers, just as it puts consumers/customers in front of organizations. If you want to confirm that the data you have is correct before you make an expensive decision, why not just ask? Th e smart organization will listen, collect responses and make the adjustments necessary to provide consumers/customers with what they require from their brand.

Driving Business Success

Two-way conversation is the gateway to smarter business success. And the outside-in thinking organization recognizes that the combination of collected data and conversation helps them to provide consumers/customers with the products/services they want—when, where and how they want them—which ultimately creates a market of willing buyers.

What more could an organization ask for?

THEHARTEOFMARKETING.com

Getting to Work

Nick Burcher

London has a complex network of public transport with different routes and different methods available to help you "get to work." Tube maps, bus maps and online journey planners help to make sense of options, whilst live updates can be obtained from a variety of sources.

"Getting to work" involves prior understanding of the system (cheapest way of travelling and quickest route) supplemented with realtime information about what is happening (delays / cancellations) and adaption to circumstances (do I need an umbrella?). You don't just blindly start out on a journey, you research it in advance and adapt, subject to updates received from live sources. Over time, personal experience then improves the journey (you learn how to get a seat, where to stop for coffee etc) and comparing actual achievements against your initial planning helps to make future journeys more effective.

In "doing social," options and routes also need to be evaluated before setting off and contingency plans should be in place to deal with unexpected problems (this may include Legal, HR, NPD as well as advertising / marketing departments). Furthermore, as with "getting to work," it is then possible to act on learning and metrics to become more effective over time — remembering that "getting to work" is a long term, regular commitment rather than a one-off.

Like the London transport map, social is a web of interlocking lines. A blog post might feed Twitter and this information could then travel further along the Twitter line. Alternatively it could change platform and travel on Facebook or it could head upstairs and start travelling over ground in a newspaper — but it might just end up at a depot not going anywhere!

RSS, sharing and linking all provide the social equivalent of a transport network, but social is more than mechanics, social is primarily about people. Social planning involves understanding consumers and the "problem" that a socialised strategy will solve (awareness, purchase, customer service or advocacy?) Listening tools help, answering "Who are the targets? What do they do? How much are they talking? What are they saying? Where are they saying it? Is it positive or negative?" With this information vital in determining optimal routes and solutions.

To "get to work," the first steps are in understanding the mechanics of the conversation *and* understanding what the audience will most appreciate — and agreeing on this before you have breakfast, let alone leave the house!

NICKBURCHER.com

Plan, Do, Measure

Karen D. Swim

Technology has transformed every facet of doing business. While not a ground-breaking revelation, the speed of innovation and adoption has driven us to reinvent business itself. We are able to automate, measure, modify and repeat with relative ease. Better still, we can now perform those tasks from the palm of our hand, thanks to smartphones and cloud computing technology. The dizzying array of tools widely available to the masses has redefined more than the nuts and bolts of business but the "how" and "why" as well. The entire ecosystem is contributory and participative, making it both inviting and intimidating. Big brands and startups have equal access to customers and customers have an equal voice to laud or decry the messages they receive.

Yet, in spite of the potential risks, the ease of access can tempt the most disciplined marketer to dive in with reckless abandon and grab their share of the conversation pie. Shoot a video, post an update, automate a few marketing messages and watch as your brilliant messaging goes viral — or will it?

The ease and efficiency of social media can disguise the need for real work. Social media with its free and low cost, shiny tools and large audiences does not eliminate the need for a good old-fashioned plan. The first step in getting to work is clearly defining what that means. Whom do you want to talk to and where are they? Mass appeal platforms will certainly have a place in your plan but do not rule out smaller niche platforms that may attract your most fervent fans. You can do as well if not better, with a small group of the right people than with a large group that is only moderately interested in what you offer.

Plan for your desired result, and measure your actions accordingly. What do you hope to gain from your efforts? What will success look like to you? Do you have the resources to allocate to the effort? The work of social media is multi-dimensional and ongoing. You are not simply distributing messaging through a marketing channel but monitoring, cultivating and engaging in conversations around that content. This applies to both your online and offline messages as you utilize social media to leverage content in all channels.

The platforms may differ but all require the roll-up-your-sleeves effort of engaging real people in real conversation.

WORDSFORHIRELLC.com

When Work Throws You a Lemon, Duck!

David Zinger, M.Ed.

When someone tells you to ***get to work*** I encourage you to **DUCK**. I believe the way to get is to let.

"Get to work" sounds dictatorial and getting things done elevates work at the expense of being who we are. I don't want to be cajoled into getting things done, not even by myself.

Rather than some sort of time-management fanaticism, I encourage you to accept these five invitations. Even if they don't succeed in getting you to work, they will ease the mental, emotional, physical, and spiritual journey to and through work. Each invitation is a quotation plus a short explanation.

1. *"You can't stop the waves but you can learn to surf."* — Jon Kabat-Zinn
   Social media sends us wave after wave of information and we can get lost in a sea of new tools. We can't stop the waves but we can learn to surf by being mindful of why we are online, what we are trying to achieve, and acceptance that the waves will sometimes takes us in new directions.

2. *"If you make where you are going more important than where you are there may be no point in going."* — Alan Watts
   Stay with some information you find before you go mindlessly linking away to the next "gem" of information. There is so much knowledge to be derived from where we are as opposed to linking our lives away.

3. *"I am not OK, you are not OK, and that's OK."* — Elisabeth Kübler-Ross
   Always remember when you run into working glitches that's OK. Don't strive so hard for some idealized social media experience and embrace mistakes.

4. *"What comes next?"* — Keith Johnstone
   This leading improvisation teacher always encouraged people to ask what comes next and to change things if they were not pleased by the answer. To ensure you like what you see about your social media future, ensure you love and embrace what comes next, or make a positive shift.

5. *"Two roads diverged in a wood, and I— I took the one less traveled by, And that has made all the difference."* — Robert Frost
   Don't be consumed by the information superhighway and let yourself be diverted as you follow your own social media pathway. Trust yourself.

When work throws you a lemon, DUCK: Develop Understanding Compassion and Kindness.

DAVIDZINGER.com

Set the Pace for Your Day Early

Daniel Sitter

Most of our activity does not necessarily generate accomplishment. How often have you arrived at the end of a busy day, exhausted from the hundred tasks that filled your agenda? Busy-ness is seldom a positive step in the pursuit of success; rather, it's often an unwelcome deterrent.

"Getting to work" is a mindset. Prior to achieving success, our desires must lead us to specifically identify the goals and methodically program the action steps necessary for their achievement. Through an active and focused process of *"plan, do and review,"* we forge forward until that very success, long-ago envisioned, is ours.

Granted, we are not machines. There will always be daily personal functions and necessary family obligations that constitute our day. These are important and must be weighed as such. If we are honest when asked about our priorities, responding with family as coming first, then we must expect to have such activities interwoven in the fabric of our day. View these as inseparable and you will avoid the guilt that often strangles your progress.

When you work, work smart. Keep distractions to a minimum. Learn to identify and prioritize tasks on your to-do list. Remember … this tool is likely to include personal items. Handle them exactly like work-related tasks. Do not unfairly burden yourself with self-imposed guilt. Handle each task in succession and keep moving forward.

The key is focus. As you wade through the hours, check-off each completed task, smile confidently and briefly savor that moment as now being one step closer to your success!

Our greatest roadblock may actually be at the beginning of each day when we face the insurmountable mountain before us and allow the crippling effects of discouragement, confusion and fear to stop us in our tracks. This is often the point at which we succumb to the excuses of activity and busy-ness as mentioned earlier. Our goals and action plans will get put on hold if we become stuck in the quicksand of indecision.

Embrace Nike's mantra, "Just Do It." Each morning, armed with goals in mind and daily to-do list in hand, jump right into your day! Don't hesitate. Set your daily pace in those early minutes. Sir Isaac Newton observed that *"an object in motion tends to stay in motion."* We too are such objects. Now get to work, pay attention and stay moving!

IDEA-SELLERS.com

Connecting with Your Advocates

Becky Carroll
||||||||||||||||||||||||||||||||||||

There are a lot of great reasons to use social media to market a business. I believe one of the most powerful reasons to market with social media is to build and strengthen customer relationships, especially with your brand advocates. This is *not* the same as creating a really cool social media campaign. Rather, this is about getting to know your customers better and empowering them to share on behalf of your brand.

The key to connecting with your brand advocates is to get them to engage with you and with each other. This is a group that is already interested in interacting with your brand and has likely self-selected by giving you access to them via email, Twitter, Facebook, communities, or all of the above. The best way to engage them is to get them talking about themselves via social media. Invite them to share a story or a photo (then to tag it so their friends will all see their interaction). Ask them something about themselves (and keep it about them, not about how much they like your brand or product). Then truly have a discussion around these areas. Dig down with your questions as if you were getting to know someone for the first time — because you are doing just that.

Where should you have this customer engagement? You can have your own "party" and invite your customers to come and join you *or* you can find out where your customers are already "partying" and go meet them there. In other words, you can invite your customers to come to your site or social media property and interact with you, or you can go and engage with them wherever they are already interacting around your brand. Either way can work, depending on your business and your customer relationships. The important thing is to get them to interact and to keep them going.

Companies that have well-established relationships with their customers will discover that social media is a great tool which complements their existing interactions. Companies that have only been using one way communication with customers will have a little work to do to get them to engage, not just once in a social media campaign, but on an ongoing basis. They should find their customers are eager and ready as long as the conversation is relevant to their needs!

||||||||||||||||||||||||||||||||||||||||||||||||||||||||||||||||||
CUSTOMERSROCK.net

Schedule It

Deb Brown
IIIIIIIIIIIIIIIIIIIIIIIIIIIIII

I got laid off from my day job in October 2008. I figured this was a good time to "get to work." It was time to learn Twitter.

The first thing I did was go to Twitter.com. I signed up for a free account and then thought, "Now what?" There was a search feature on Twitter and I used it. I typed in "social media." I started reading conversations between people. Some had less of an idea than I did. Others were giving links for me to read, smart advice and were answering questions. It was those people I followed. Then I started to follow the people they followed. If you think one guy is pretty smart — wouldn't his friends probably be smart too? I finally got up enough nerve to join in a few conversations. I asked a lot of questions. If someone said something smart, I retweeted it. I shared links. I spent about two weeks developing a social media community all for me on twitter.

Today, I check my Twitter account throughout the day. I use TweetDeck for organization. If I'm at an event, I tweet it. I take pictures and share them. I spend about an hour a day looking for people who want to talk to me. I use the search features to see who is looking for better health and a safer home environment.

Many things have happened because of Twitter. I went on a blogging tour to Hutchinson, KS — that got my name out in the field, and I met amazing bloggers. I attended SobCon09 by getting sponsors locally, based on suggestions by Twitter associates. I've added new members to my team. I've gotten speaking engagements; made lots of new business connections; and written guest blog posts for Twitter friends. Twitter has taught me more about social media than I ever thought possible — and it's been a conversation in 140 characters!

Set up a schedule. It's easy to get lost in Twitter world and a schedule holds you accountable to your business. Make a commitment of 12 or 24 months to use Twitter as a marketing tool. It does not happen overnight usually. Don't profess to be something you're not, be transparent and tell the truth. Share — don't shove your business down people's throats. Every 13th tweet can be about your business — the rest are conversations. Have fun!

IIIIIIIIIIIIIIIIIIIIIIIIIIIIIIIIIIIIIIIIIIIII
DEBWORKS.com

The Social Networking Superhighway

Carol Bodensteiner

Years ago, I attended a six-week long workshop in New York. Participants represented countries all over the world. For many, English was a difficult second language. At the end of the six weeks, English remained an insurmountable barrier for some. For others, English was no longer a hurdle; they participated easily in all discussions. A Brazilian man who fell into the second group described it this way:

> *"Learning to speak English is like sitting in a car at the side of a freeway. Watching from the shoulder, the cars go by incredibly fast. But once you ease into traffic, the other cars don't seem to be going as fast. Gradually you pick up speed and pretty soon, you're going as fast as they are."*

The analogy of easing into traffic and picking speed applies to social networking tools as well. The challenges of new technology can seem overwhelming, particularly for someone who grew up as I did, building my career on typewriters and fax machines. When the internet came on the scene, I thought to myself — *Maybe I can retire before I have to learn this.* No kidding, that's what I thought.

Traffic on the internet moved so quickly, I could only watch from the side of the road for a time. Gradually, I eased onto the highway. I created my blog and wrote entries — testing my voice, experimenting with style, and deciding whether I could sustain content — for a full year before telling anyone.

Sometimes I pulled off in frustration. I lurked around Facebook, opened an account, closed it in exasperation. Then tried again.

Gradually, I've picked up speed, following a social networking roadmap marking the way to a business presence. Strategies include Facebook and LinkedIn postings that position me as a resource for writing or communication strategy, blog entries that show my writing style and depth. Tweets? Still the fast lane. I'm watching.

I've learned from others, asked for and received help, watched writers who are skilled social networkers, and adopted techniques that suit my needs and style. It surprises no one so much as me that others now ask for my advice.

Adopting my Brazilian friend's approach, I turned on to the social networking superhighway, inched along for a while, learned and picked up speed, and now I'm cruising along as I Get to Work.

CAROLBODENSTEINER.com

How Social Media Aids the Job-Seeker

Suzanne Hull

As a person who was laid off in 2009 (twice), I began using social media as a tool during my job search.

In May, I started a blog about being unemployed in Des Moines; I had a lot on my mind and my husband was tired of listening. I also thought that by sharing my experiences during this difficult time with others who were going through the same thing, we might be able to learn from each other. Through this process, I discovered my flair for writing and learned how to develop and write a blog. These efforts drew a lot of attention from the Des Moines community and hiring managers.

Getting a Twitter account has been the best thing that I could have done to aid in my job search. After learning Twitter etiquette, I dove in and with the help of TweetDeck, I'm able to manage my Twitter stream. My Twitter handle is @unemployedindsm, so you can imagine the types of users who follow me and vice versa. I follow job boards, career coaches, employment agencies, staffing firms, recruiters, etc, and make use of the hash tag search feature that is available. I have also been privy to job openings posted only by the people I follow on Twitter; their company doesn't post job openings on job boards.

One's social media presence needs to be managed properly, especially during the job search. Google yourself; this is what your potential employer sees. Your LinkedIn profile needs to be completed. Protect your Facebook profile if you don't want all of your private information viewable by the general public. Create a Google profile and include information in it that you want to share with someone who Googles you. There are ways you can take control of your online presence.

Needless to say, the type of job I was looking for has changed dramatically over the past several months, due to my involvement with social media and the relationships I've developed with its users. As soon as I moved the laptop from the couch in the basement to the kitchen table upstairs, I started getting some real work done. Sometimes all it takes is a change of scenery to get busy.

UNEMPLOYEDINDESMOINES.com

Start with a Cup of Social Coffee

Anibal Casso

|||||||||||||||||||||||||||||||||

Want to make the most out of social media in your everyday work life? Let's start by losing the script.

I have learned that, when used properly, one of the main strengths of social media is its inherent ability to help enhance productivity. Beyond the predictable benefits of interacting with others, at its core, it opens a door to an entire world of possibilities that range from the basic tools to more complex new methods. But, in order to achieve this, it becomes crucial to wipe out all the bias we have regarding social media and embrace it as something more organic.

The past two years have been living proof of social media's influence on the way we work. Many have leveraged it as a valuable source of information through the numerous links shared on a daily basis. Others simply use it as a reliable source for inspiration. The truth is, no matter the reason, we can achieve much more just by harnessing social networking's power. Using tweets and posts can organically spark new takes on the very same ideas we started with.

But, hold it right there. It looks great on paper, but how do we make it actionable?

Start with your morning coffee.

By starting the day diving into the social media pool, we tap into the thoughts of infinite creative minds that remind us how rewarding it's to break with the *status quo*. Once you turn on your social radar before getting to work, you get in touch with a fresh wave of resourceful voices that will inspire you along the way.

A single morning sip of your daily reader will show you that when you apply social media as a thinking device, it helps you evolve your own ideas, craft stronger points of view and discover tangible methods of bringing these to life. Literally.

The bottom line is that we should all look to the social media toolkit as a continual reminder that we are part of a collective and that, in essence, we all have something valuable to share. The goal is to take all that richness and make it part of an ongoing social school of thinking that, on a daily basis, launches us into un-chartered territories.

Seriously, getting to work is much easier when we start with a cup of social coffee.

|||||||||||||||||||||||||||||||||||||||||||||||||||||||||||||||||

ACCIDENTALTHINKING.com

Being Human

Dennis Deery
ıllıllıllıllıllıllıllıllıllıllıllıllıll

I sit down at my desk and fire up my computer. First stop is my email, the original social media. This is my 21st-century direct phone line. It's the main point of contact from clients, family and friends that have yet to drink the social media Kool-Aid.

Next, I fire up TweetDeck to check Twitter. I currently live in the United States, but have also spent some time living in Ireland. A morning check of Twitter keeps me up-to-date with the kind of day my Irish friends have had. Twitter is also my main source for breaking news (confesses the political junkie), and is a great source for reminders of social events, training events, etc. Twitter has even been a source of projects for my consulting company when friends or colleagues have tweeted a need for assistance.

Finally, my morning routine is complete with a check of updates from LinkedIn and Facebook, using Google Reader to aggregate the updates. So far Facebook has been entirely social for me. LinkedIn keeps me on top of the professional happenings in my network. The Q&A section is a great source of information, and a place to build additional contacts by answering questions.

Social media is scattered throughout the rest of my day as well. I use Google Reader to stay on top of all kinds of news, and am just beginning to explore the social features. I regularly post bookmarks to Delicious, where they are then fed to my blog.

So what do I gain from all this activity? As an independent consultant, I need to maintain as much of a presence in the lives of my network as possible. The crumbs I scatter across these sites are trails that potential clients can follow to find me.

More importantly, we should remember that "social media" is not new stuff. The "media" we're using is new, but the "social" is a base part of being human. We have an inherent need to connect with other humans, to belong to a community, however we define that community. In this age when so many of us work alone, at home, these new tools allow us to make and maintain so many of the incidental connections that others, working out in the world, just get as part of their normal day. We are simply using new technology to be human!

ıllıllıllıllıllıllıllıllıllıllıllıllıllıllıllıllıllıllıllıllıll

DENNISDEERY.com

Stop Talking at People

Rich Nadworny

What is it about marketing that makes perfectly normal people (well, most of us anyway) lose their ability to speak like a human being? If you spoke to the people you know in the same way you write your promotional material, they'd look at you like you're crazy. If you do this in social media people will simply ignore you. To find success in social media, you'll need to learn how to speak and write normally, again.

Most people and businesses that jump into social media stumble at this. One client of mine is passionate about old cars. He's part of a national club and arranged for his company to sponsor and host one of the club's major events. He even put together a special product promotion to highlight and celebrate the event. When he told me all about this his eyes glittered, his hands punctuated his sentences and he even gave a little hop or two. That's how energized and excited he was.

And then he said, "So, I'd like to post this on Facebook and Twitter. Can I say, 'Old Car Super Special'? '3 for 2'? Or, '50% on second purchase!'?"

I told him, "No." No-one wants to hear his sales pitch. We want to hear and share his excitement. We want to listen to his story. My advice to him, and others jumping into social media, is to communicate and write like you talk. It takes practice. Writing with emotion and personality are key to social media. When people feel like you're talking *with* them and not *at* them, they won't tune out so quickly. Talking with people gives them an opportunity to respond, add things on, and pass on the story.

Here's a quick task — take all of your marketing and promotional material and turn it into talk. How would you tell your best friend about this? Or your mother? Practice writing like you speak, and use that tone on social media. Speak as if you expect a response.

You should also set up a system to pull in all the examples when you talk at your customer and not with them. Gather them up, share them with your marketing group, ask everyone to rewrite one or two, and then stand up and present the changes. When you've finished laughing, post them on your social media channels.

It might spark some great conversations.

DIGITALSTRATEGY.TYPEPAD.com

The Tie Which Binds:
Learning Is the New Currency

Heather Rast

In Tom Rath's bestselling book *StrengthsFinder 2.0*, he presents assessments of 34 separate talent themes he believes represent the spectrum of human intellectual and emotional complexity.

By overlaying those themes with traits demonstrated by active members of social communities, it seems several areas are held in common; one relates to learning, a driving appetite for information.

According to Rath, people possessing this theme are drawn to the process of learning, the "steady and deliberate journey from ignorance to competence."* Learners are insatiably curious and inquisitive, intrigued by many (and often diverse) topics, and very receptive to new concepts.

Learners can bring comfort to others, drawing them into new subjects and simplifying the complex. The subject matter authority garnered by learners, coupled with their enthusiasm and passion for topics, can fuel teams and inspire followers. Learners are propelled to discover, process, digest, and disburse.

Learners take pleasure in soaking up ideas, knowledge, and experience and re-distributing our learnings for others to enjoy or benefit by. Our technology-enabled world is one where distance and time blur, relationships form organically, and introductions are an intrinsic function of participation. Here, the gift of information is everyone's to share.

When we talk about creating value for our network, of being additive and generous, I think we're really driving toward sharing what we know, what we've learned, to share the beauty of *knowing* with those who matter. Being helpful, encouraging viewpoints and debate; facilitating informed decisions. We've set up our metaphorical store front and set about delivering our informational wares. We share in order to enjoy repeat visitors and an engagement that fuels positive word of mouth (learners appreciate audiences; the more we enlighten, aid and touch, the better). In old times, it (learning) may have been centered around tribe preservation, security, or being efficient and economical with resources. But today I believe an ever-increasing supply of tools necessitates that we hold these nascent, yet promising, relationships dear, and use the information made available to bridge gaps in commerce and foster communities of selfless problem solvers.

Some tools have become popular, still others are emerging as early adoption gives rise to acceptance and mainstreaming. Here we rest in this fragile environment, situated between understanding and scale. We need motivated learners to produce and discover the content that binds our common interests and values, enabling the informational exchange connecting people, personality, and perspective.

* Tom Rath, *Strengths Finder 2.0*, Gallup Press, 2007, p 133.

INSIGHTSANDINGENUITY.com

Creativity

Leah Otto

Fundamentals remain the same, but the tools change so quickly. How to keep up? Just as an athlete stays in shape, it helps if you're always ready.

Here are three things you can do to keep your social media instincts strong:

1. Always be experimenting
2. Honor your creative ideas everyday
3. Listen.

Always Be Experimenting

If you are in the habit of exploring new mediums, you will find them easier to use when pressured to try something new.

Make it a goal to adopt new communications tools as they come up. There are so many that no one can do them all. But if you're constantly exploring, you'll be closer to your audiences. You'll have a better idea of what will stick when you need to reach them.

Honor Your Creative Ideas

Social media requires innovative thinking. Audiences respond to fresh approaches, so when you want to start a social media campaign, your creativity needs to be ready. But if you rarely let your ideas out, it could feel awkward to suddenly need ideas. Take ten minutes each day to empty your brain with free flow writing. Doodle. Cook something new. It doesn't have to be big. It doesn't have to be for anything important. But *doing* it is important because you need to get your ideas *out*.

Think about it. All day long we're taking ideas *in*. We're on the internet, we're catching the news, we're briefed on new clients. Experts on creativity say if you don't take time to get your ideas *out*, then you *will* be blocked when you need an idea fast.

Think of it as energy. It has to keep moving. It has to keep flowing. If not, it will become stale and stagnant.

Listen

The third and final way to jump start your ability to get to work is to listen. Listen for what your audience needs. Listen for how your audience can be reached. Are they on Twitter? Would it be better to go with mobile phone messaging? Are they blogging? Are they talking about your company? What are they saying? Do they need help? Do they have complaints?

Listening helps define your project. The more clearly defined you are, the better you know how to maximize your resources. Listening is critical to setting yourself up for success.

SCRIBBLESANDSTRAYS.WORDPRESS.com

Will You Matter?

Leigh Duncan-Durst

The truth is this — social media and Web 2.0 tools are merely a means to an end. Creating a truly meaningful experience — one that matters to prospects, customers, competitors, the business and even society — is the next brand differentiator *and* success indicator. So, before we get to work, each of us must answer this simple question: **"How is this going to matter?"**

This isn't lofty thinking — it's pragmatic. And, while it's true that businesses use conversational media and tools in different ways, answering this question *should* become an easy exercise. Here are just a few examples of how conversational media and tools matter to businesses <u>and</u> every day people.

Better Serving People	Extending service and response to dynamic new channels	Providing helpful, relevant product &/or service updates	Responding proactively to direct & indirect feedback	Removing barriers that impact decision making & transactions	Understanding people & their needs.	Rewarding participation & loyalty
Listening, Learning & Applying	Proactively listening & responding to direct / indirect feedback	Accepting criticism with grace, humility & stewardship	Leveraging feedback to improve products & services	Sourcing ideas and feedback from "the crowd"	Adding new value-add features	Finding new audiences and uses for your products or services
Improving Business Operations	Improving distribution of information, interaction	Streamlining key tasks & introducing new efficiencies	Responding faster, better and more efficiently	Mobilizing quickly to capitalize on market & competitive opportunity	Improving organizational communication	Breaking down operational silos
Driving & facilitating high-value transactions	Building a thriving, growing & targeted network	Fostering active dialog & engagement	Increasing online &/or offline traffic	Driving conversions, leads & sales	Resolving issues that negatively impact customer experience	Taking brand evangelists to the next level
Creating a personal, intimate experience	Connecting with people in the channels they use most for life & work	Personally recognizing people, accomplishments & innovation	Responding to people, the market & competitors with a human voice	Motivating people to experience products & services	Engaging & encouraging participation in giving & social good	Jointly celebrating milestones, events & successes

Creating a conversational presence that matters requires focus across all the areas above — not just one. Make sure your social, digital, conversational presence matters. If you already have a plan that doesn't include the elements above — regroup, retrench and reformulate. Use the **"Does this Matter"** question to focus your daily activities. Adopting this focus will create a growing, thriving network that drives bottom line results.

Taking Twitter Face-to-Face

Lesley Lambert

For me the power of social media has been in finding local people on Twitter, getting to know them via their tweets, and then taking our friendship face-to-face.

I use TwitterLocal (see TwitterLocal.com), an Adobe Air application, to discover people near me, by zipcode. You can also use Twitter's search. It is my practice to try to follow everyone in my region and engage them over a common topic. This has been a very effective technique both for making new friends and for finding new clients for my real estate business.

Last year I made the acquaintance of a lovely couple from my town on Twitter. Later, we met in real life at PodCamp Western Massachusetts, and it was at that face-to-face meeting that they mentioned they had a home to sell. We continued our friendship on Facebook as well as Twitter, and a short while later they asked to meet with me. Over coffee, they asked me if I could work as their real estate agent. They told me that they had observed how I represented myself and my clients through social media and they liked what they saw. I was able to sell their house quickly, and in addition, we remain very good friends.

As my own experience illustrates, Twitter has incredible power as a pre-qualification tool for people in all types of business. It allows you to find potential customers in your area, or by keyword, and then to create a relationship with them. Once that relationship is established, if they like you and trust you, they are then more likely to use your service or product.

It is important to realize that potential clients are screening you via your social media interactions and to bear that in mind when posting online. Everyone has a different idea of what their social media "voice" should be. For me, I am very comfortable sharing my life online — I have used social media to reach out to people as a single mom, realtor, dance instructor, friend and social media teacher. My voice online is consistent with my voice offline — outgoing, friendly, energetic and sometimes sarcastic. Sharing my true self online has brought me an amazing partner, business and friends all over the world.

Twitter by itself is a great tool for business, but when you combine Twitter with face-to-face meetings, you tap into a whole new level of networking for your business.

TWITTERQUEENS.net

Getting to Work

Mark Price

Getting to work is more than putting words on a screen.

Getting to work is not busy-work or lazy-work or fill-in-the-time work.

Getting to work is a conscientious commitment to engaging a community in discussion, with valuable insight frequently delivered.

Getting to work encompasses two different issues — consistency and finding the right social media channel and messages for your business.

Let's Get At It

The only way to make a new strategy important is to make it a priority and work at it consistently. Consistency means a weekly schedule. My goal is to write every week from 2–6 pm on Sunday. By allocating a fixed time for original writing, I keep the act in focus. For comments on other people's material, I write as soon as I get into the office. That way, this work gets done before the day (and my clients) heat up. What gets started first, gets finished.

Making It Work

Focus is the key to making social media work, focusing on the right social media channels and delivering the right messages. First, you need to determine which channels attract your target audience. Do you want to speak to teens? Then don't use Twitter, which has low teen participation rates. If you want to speak to moms, then Facebook is more appropriate, since the fastest-growing demographic on Facebook is moms.

Remember, if your customers and recommenders are not active on social networking, then you may be wasting your time by participating in any of these platforms.

For me, my target community (marketing executives) read blogs and participate on LinkedIn. So I began with a consistent weekly blog. By adding my blog to my LinkedIn profile, my effort writing the blog is multiplied. I build my presence with my contacts by adding one or two recommendations on LinkedIn per week and commenting on a LinkedIn group weekly.

What do I write about? What my community is talking about, of course. *Not* what I want to sell them — social media is not about selling as much as about content marketing and conversations. Stay focused on helping out, and don't worry about compensation — customers will engage with you soon enough.

So in summary, "Getting to Work" is:

A consistent discipline to reaching customers and prospects, in their preferred social media channel, providing valuable, trust-building content and contributing to conversations.

Enough talk, let's get to work.

BLOGS.MSQUAREDGROUP.com

"I Get To!" Get to Work

Joan Endicott
||||||||||||||||||||||||||||||||||||||||

Thomas Jefferson said, "I never believed there was one code of morality for a public [man], and another for a private man."

My heart goes out to those who've said or done something they wish they hadn't and can't take it back — then it became public. Whether in a business setting, sports event or even private forum, a video of it may end up on YouTube. It seems there are always plenty of examples of individuals who've "lost it," made poor choices or had a moment of venting or compromise — which then becomes public. Whether in mainstream media or any of the various opportunities for social networking, once a person says, writes or does something, though he or she may regret it, it can't be undone.

As a professional speaker and consultant, a reoccurring concern clients have is their employees wasting valuable company time, energy and resources on various social networking — not for promoting the business, but for their own personal promotion and enjoyment. The amount of time and money stolen from employers through this media is incalculable.

In business, these tools should be used to insure a benefit to the business; high visibility, increased advertising, branding and marketing opportunities.

It also should be used to enhance and compliment the communication they already have with customers and potential customers, adding value to those relationships.

Having integrity means using these tools to "get to work" at work, in order to enhance your business and professional relationships, period!

Warning: Just in case nobody's told you yet … on any technology device once you hit "send," IT'S NOT PRIVATE, you have lost control — forever. It can end up with anyone, anywhere, any time — worldwide.

A great rule to live by, if there's any doubt — throw it out. Don't say it, write it or send it. If you wouldn't want it on the six o' clock news or the front of the morning paper, don't communicate it in any way.

Whether using social networking for professional and/or personal use, never compromise. A moment of compromise is never worth the price it demands.

I've never met anyone who regretted having too high of standards, yet have met thousands who regretted lowering theirs.

> *"The time is always right to do the right thing."*
> — Martin Luther King

||||||||||||||||||||||||||||||||||||||||||||||||||
JOANENDICOTT.com

Re/Start with Strong Social Media Character

Wayne Buckhanan

Do you recognize these common characters from social media sites?

Link Lobbers — may really be robots. There is little or no interaction, just announcements. Commonly they haven't been on the site in months because their auto posting tools "make life easier."
Self Distracters — luvz yer lolcats. They may bump your stats while you serve up something entertaining but interaction is limited to "lol," "roflmao," and/or "me too!"
Ego Strokers — need the biggest number. Be it friends, followers, contacts, or subscribers. Often spotted making random friend requests or sending "invite blast" emails to their whole address book.

Which One Are You?

Fortunately, while these three make up the majority, there is another option available. Unfortunately, due to the requirements, genuine **Servant-Leaders** are few and far between.
Problem: No-one seems to care.
Apathy will kill your forward progress — whether it is in your personal life, the causes you support, or your business network.
Solution: Put the social back in the medium!
People **don't** care about big numbers. Everyone wants to be part of something bigger than themselves, but they don't **connect** because of shouting or a sales pitch.
People care about people. They connect through interaction with another person. The way to develop connections rather than just increase numbers is by building rapport with your audience and listening to what they are passionate about.

Get Started Connecting

There are three distinct ways to develop those connections: build new relationships, maintain current relationships, or renew lapsed relationships.
Each of these requires a slightly different approach in terms of presumptions, tone, frequency, and content. However, they all share the same need for listening to everybody's favorite radio station: **WIIFM**.
"What's In It For Me" isn't about you. It's about your audience. This is where listening, empathy, and understanding build the foundation of the connection. And this is where the **Servant-Leader** shines — developing relationships in social media, corporate culture, and with friends and family.

Get Started Today

Whether through diligent practice or a solid course in **Neuro-Linguistic Programming (NLP)** every one of us can cultivate the communication skills that make a real difference: empathetic rapport, flexibility of perspective, and a win-win or no deal attitude.
Start honing your skills — break the apathy today by listening to someone else's **WIIFM** and connect as a person. You may even build a reputation as a **Servant-Leader!**

LIFELOVEANDLEARNING.com/blog

Checking Off My Day

Mike Maddaloni

As I head to my morning appointment, I am going against the tide. It is me versus thousands pouring out of the train station, heading to their offices. As they make their way towards me, I am not sure they actually see me. I am not in disguise as much as they are. Some are hiding behind a cup of coffee. Others are covered in a digital shroud tied at the top with white headphones. More are dressed right out of Michael Jackson's *Thriller* video — zombies that could probably use coffee and music. Their path is one they must take, but it sure doesn't look like they want to be taking it.

Though I am off to my appointment, I did not start my day with a commute to work like them. That is, unless you count the 10 paces from my bedroom to my home office via the kitchen for a cup of coffee. This has been my path to the headquarters of my internet consultancy for the last half decade when I first went out on my own. There are advantages and surely disadvantages to having a home office, and having no commute whatsoever is certainly a big check in the pluses column.

Working from home is by no means a perfect scenario. It requires discipline, which automatically comes with a commute. You need to shut down. You need to get on with the rest of your life. You need to have fun, with fun defined as something not related to work. It is tougher as an entrepreneur, where what you do is so intertwined into your life. It can define it, or worse — it can be the third wheel in your relationship. These are certainly checks in the negative column.

After getting to my appointment, I paused and reflected on how I got there. The faces of the people I passed looked withdrawn. Sure, the economy could be part of it. Certainly they could be literal zombies in search of caffeine. These thoughts, however, were quickly interrupted by someone, my daughter. She wanted out of the stroller I just pushed her in, taking her to swimming lessons. Now that I think of it, maybe some of those faces were in surprise of a Dad pushing along his daughter. In any case, it is a great feeling I have the flexibility where I can take her to the pool. Both of these facts are more checks in the pluses column.

THEHOTIRON.com

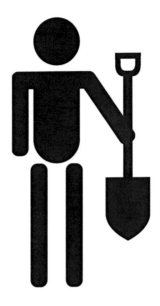

Pitching Social Media

New World of Media Calls for Old Pitching Rules

David Reich

Newspapers are dying, magazines are going online and no one watches TV in realtime. The changes in the media world are unlike anything we've ever witnessed.

Or are they?

The hype, accurate or not, gets amplified by the fact that anyone with a computer or a web-enabled cell phone can put their own thoughts out there for all to read, unfettered by an editor or by space limitations. So we start to believe that it truly is a brave new media world, with a new set of rules. It's easy to be convinced that this new order demands that public relations pros use new tech-inspired protocols for reaching out to the media.

The reality, however, is that the same basic rules for pitching media 30 years ago are equally applicable today.

Targeting
PR people must do their homework. The internet makes it easier to find targets, but it still takes research. Even with online media resource guides, you must be familiar with media *before* you pitch them. It's time-consuming, but read and become familiar with what each media target covers.

Think Like an Editor
PR people need to remember it's not about what they want publicized; it's about what the editor, producer or blogger feels is of interest to his or her audience. Put yourself in the editor's head to figure out what he might want. If you can't come up with an angle to honestly make your material of interest to the editor's audience, you need to come up with a different story idea, get more relevant information or drop that editor from your target list.

Waste the media's time with off-target pitches and that editor probably won't take your calls or emails in the future.

Pitch Succinctly
Make it brief and to the point. Explain why your idea is relevant to your target's audience. If you're calling, ask first if this is a good time for the person to talk. If the editor's mind is on something else, your chances of success drop dramatically.

Learn How to Take "No" For an Answer
If an editor says your idea isn't right for him, you might gently try a different approach, but don't badger and plead. Accept "no" gracefully and you'll have a chance with that editor for another idea in the future.

It's a new media world. But some old, common sense pitching rules still work.

REICHCOMM.TYPEPAD.com

"You're Selling the Wrong Thing"

Aki Spicer

The thrill of the "new" has caused many of us to pitch our social ideas based on the wrong strategies and arguments. We wrapped social media in alarmism and fear, and/or the sheer "gee-whiz" tech novelty of it all. The aftermath — post-purchase dissonance, confusion and backlash against the "social media guru."

The fatal flaw of these bad sales approaches: you're selling social ideas as a technology or tactic, a new, shiny box to check off—not a strategy to solve business problems. In short, *you're selling the wrong thing.*

Not Art or Technologies — Answers and Solutions

Understandably, "tweets," "virals," "widgets," and "diggs" can seem like frivolous artistic indulgences. Your clients don't seek to buy art. Art = risks, and clients don't want to buy risks. However, they are desperate to buy answers and solutions to their problems.

So stop selling the wrong thing and sell them solutions.

Even at the user-end, people seek answers and solutions — not your social arts and technologies. The users, the customers, the people — they simply want to reach their goals better, faster, easier. And, if you have better-faster-easier to offer, then they may lend you a click and a "digg."

So, give people what they want — solutions to their problems.

Insights In. Insights Out

If you don't have insights into the problems, you're selling the wrong thing.

All good ideas start with an insight into what people want and need. Without an insight, you're not likely to be relevant to users' needs. And without setting up the insights into a problem, your clients don't have the framework to judge and buy your ideas.

Insights — go get 'em. Then help clients see your social idea as an insight-driven solution to their issues.

Embrace Data

If you're not leveraging web data to sell your social idea, you're selling the wrong thing.

Brand managers with MBAs rely on accounting rationale and statistical rigor. Clients want ideas grounded by data. So embrace data.

Turn your data into insights. Let insights drive your ideation. Develop your ideas, release them to users, then measure more data to evolve the ideas into things that clients want to buy.

Sell What Clients Want to Buy

A few years into this social thing, and it has become clear that clients most want to buy clear and measurable results. So, it's time we all stop selling the wrong things and sell our clients results.

FALLON.com/fallon-blog

From Pitch to Participate — A New Model for Social Media Relations

Kevin Dugan

When discussing best practices in media relations, public relations professionals tend to focus on incremental improvements. Massive amounts of time and energy are spent discussing details like how to best format and distribute content.

In the meantime, larger issues, like the difference between pitching mainstream media and pitching social media influentials (SMI), go ignored. Sifting through a combined 12 years of pitches sent to Strategic Public Relations (see prblog.typepad.com) and The Bad Pitch Blog (see badpitch.blogspot.com), it's clear that significant changes must take place for successful social media outreach.

Different Audiences, Different Motivations

The most obvious difference between the media and SMI? Motivation. While reporters enter the field of journalism inspired and passionate — it's their job. As a result, some reporters simply put up with ham-fisted or off-target pitches.

SMI are inspired to create content about their passion and distribute it online. And it's a labor of love as most of them are not getting paid to blog, tweet, share links and post videos. As a result they take it very personally if a PR person sends them an off-target pitch. It's an offense against their passion.

The Social Media Paradox

This motivation plays into a social media paradox. While sites allow us to update content 24x7x365 from anywhere with a Wi-Fi signal, SMI have a day job that takes precedence over content creation. They aren't on deadline so, if blogging conflicts with real work or real play, they can stop creating content. This causes issues for PR people taking a strict, campaign approach to outreach. More time is needed when trying to engage SMI.

Using a Different Model

A different model is needed for social media outreach. Instead of pitching as a part of a media relations campaign, perhaps we should be participating as a part of a community relations commitment?

The goal of most community relations efforts is to become a member of a community by educating and informing them of your client's work. This takes more time, but the potential outcome is well worth it.

As traditional media outlets continue to lose their audience, they're losing relevance for media relations campaigns. By engaging social media influentials in conversation, you'll do more than create content and impact search. In some cases you'll go from placing one story to creating loyal advocates that will help your clients reach their goals.

PRBLOG.TYPEPAD.com

Begin at the End

Tiphereth Gloria

2009 may go down in history as the year when social hit mainstream. Clients are now seriously considering or throwing social in the deep end as a part of their marketing mix. The best social pieces are the long term campaigns which, to me, result in creating social brands, while short term campaigns may relate to causes or tactical responses — but there is a common pitch process to both.

Every great pitch tells a story, and there is reverse logic in beginning at the imagined end of a social campaign. What does the social brand look like? What results have you achieved? How have they related back to the business objectives? How has it related to other marketing activity? How are we solving the clients' biggest problem? By imagining or defining the future, we can help take the clients on a journey, and take their brand to a place they had never imagined before.

The end or the objectives of the social campaign is the stake in the ground. We must build on this framework to create the rest of the pitch document. I like to do a mini-audit and check what the clients' competitors are up to, what the industry looks like and what people are saying about the brand, and where they are saying it. The analysis and output of social media monitoring tools help win pitches because they show the conversations are already taking place — mostly without the client.

The filler is the process — how do we get to where we want to be and what channels and tactical approaches do we need to take to get there? Why is one channel more important than another? What are the reasons people like to talk about brands in social media? Clients like it if it relates to something they understand previously — the more the social influence marketing process is explained in everyday language, the more trust is built between you and the client.

I use a social process diagram to illustrate the process milestones and then break it down to key deliverables and a timeline. This is what we are going to do for you and this is how long it's going to take. It's also important to articulate what kind of a commitment you need from your client — as money/ budget may not be enough. Your clients' commitment to undertake the social journey is the most important. Because social requires stamina — it's best to explain that results may not be instant, but they will be really worthwhile.

I'm very practical when it comes to delivering social pitches. So my summary is:

- Begin at the end — what will be the results?
- Monitor and/or audit the brand — it will help you choose which channel to engage with
- Define the scope of the project and list the deliverables
- Explain the process
- Get a commitment from the client

Cross your fingers and hope you get it. Learn from the pitch process, re-read your presentation, refine and repeat.

DIGITALTIP.com.au

Forget the Muzzle — Put a Saddle on It

Mike Sansone

I remember when I graduated high school about 30 years ago. I asked my Dad for an email account. Of course, as any Dad back then would say (while nodding his loving head), "A what?" It didn't exist — but now everyone has one, even the kids.

People have been trying to connect in stronger, better, faster ways for years. Building better relationships, sharing ideas, having meaningful conversations.

From the Pony Express to the telegraph; from the telephone to fax machines; from blogging to geo-tagging — it's in our nature to connect. Tools change, the desire for touch doesn't.

Let's realize the first name in the titles of social media and social networking is "social" —and our reach, speed and variety of tools is greater than ever before. And it's possible we haven't seen nothin' yet!

I really do remember my grandparents telling me, at one point, they thought the telephone would ruin relationships because it would replace face-to-face meetings.

Maybe that's the crutch of social media. People are scared that computers will replace the face-to-face. But as all the previous instances of new connectivity tools have proven, face-to-face can actually (and should be) enhanced.

- Small talk at meetings become bigger, because much of the chitter-chatter ("How are things going?" "What's new?") is often already seen or heard via social tools
- Engagement online is deeper because of the face-to-face meetings
- Introductions are made by either handshakes or hyperlinks
- Commonality is recognized easily by social sharing tools.

Not all social media tools may be right for your company or conversation, but with as much as is out there, there is a tool that will increase your opportunities to connect and amplify your voice, your relationships, your network.

Stop trying to muzzle the conversation.

The horse is out of the barn. Saddle her up and enjoy the ride. This ain't the Pony Express anymore.

CONVERSTATIONS.com

Pitching? Let Social Media Monitoring Lead the Way

Mark Goren

If you're pitching social media to a client, throw them into it. No, I'm not suggesting that you force them to do something that they're not familiar or comfortable with. I'm merely suggesting that you show them just how much they're already in social media — whether they realize it or not.

Though many brand-level folk think that they're still in control of corporate messaging, they're not. Online conversations are taking place about their brand with or without their knowledge, with or without their consent. However, with even just a basic understanding of some social media monitoring tools, you can show clients what people are saying about their brands.

Let's assume you have an RSS reader and know how to subscribe to search engine result feeds. (If not, just ask and I'll be happy to walk you through the process.)

To start, take a defined period of time, say a week or two up to a month, and start keeping an eye on what's being said about a specific client-related brand or the company itself.

Once that's set up, watch for the following:

- What are people saying — is it good, bad, indifferent?
- Is there a story that has emerged that your client should be aware of? Look for customer service opportunities or reputation issues.
- Where is the conversation originating from? A particular website? Blogger? Twitter?
- Anything else that may be pertinent to your client given your understanding of their unique environment.

Once you have a handle on the story, there are different ways of presenting the information to the client. To begin, show your client how you'd use the information to plan new marketing initiatives. Whether for offline or online strategies, the information you're collecting should be used to help guide your planning.

Think about it.

You're going to learn a lot about the issues and lingo being used in relation to the brand or competitive environment. If you're responsible for developing offline messages, you can reflect some of what you're learning back to the audience in an effort to be more responsive and conversational in printed or broadcast material. Online, you can use the information to show your client how to respond to or initiate online conversations.

In either case, you're using social media to make your client smarter, more responsive or, at minimum, better in tune with their customers.

So go ahead, pitch that.

SOCIALMEDIAMONITORING.ca
PLANTINGSEEDS.ca

Your Mother Doesn't Pitch Here Anymore …

Nettie Hartsock

If you're still operating on the misguided notion that social media is not here to stay, or even worse, that it is not a viable option for PR pitching, then step away from this chapter and by all means go back to playing with your mint condition *Atari Pong Game*.

If, however, you do understand that social media is vibrant, ever-increasing and valuable, then keep reading!

Today's lesson is about pitching and social media. What follows are some tips for you to employ if you really want to find the best possible places to pitch yourself, your products or your brand online.

1. Don't pitch on social media platforms where you don't have a presence. Set up your Facebook fan page, your blog, your Twitter account, and shine up your LinkedIn.com profile as well.
2. Don't push out generic pitches to anyone and everyone on these accounts.
3. Do your research and don't mass pitch lists of folks. This is really a no-no on social media platforms.
4. Don't write your pitches with you in mind, write them with the producer, blogger or journalist in mind.
5. Practice makes perfect. There is something incredibly valuable about learning to pitch a brand or product in less than 140 characters.
6. Don't pitch a journalist or a blogger more than three times if you've not yet had a response from them.
7. If they ask you to stop pitching them — really do.
8. Don't Twitter-stalk journalists or bloggers.
9. If you cannot fit your pitch into 140 characters or less, rework it until you can.
10. Always follow-up with a thank you if a blogger or Twitterer shares your news with their readership.

Bonus: Five Ways to Not Twitter-Pitch Oprah

1. Hey O, this is Melanie and I want to be on your show.
2. Hey O, for Oprah's picks — what could be better than a nail polish with a fungicide included as an ingredient?
3. Hey O, your magazine sucks without me in it.
4. Hey O, I'm a publicist and I will lose my job unless I can get our client's bodice ripping romance book as a pick on your show.
5. Hey O, I created cupcakes for you and Kirstie Alley that are diuretics, so no matter how many you eat, you will still lose weight.

NETTIEHARTSOCK.com

How to Convince Your Boss of the Importance of Blogs

Charles Sipe

When most business people think of social media marketing, they think of Twitter and Facebook, and forget about the most effective social media tool for most businesses — the blog. Convincing your boss that a blog is a valuable marketing asset to invest in, however, can be a challenge. Many managers and Fortune 100 CEOs are resistant to the idea, which is not suprising considering that, as of June 2009, none of them have blogs. (see www.uberceo.com/ceoslackers). There are two major reasons every company should have a blog — blogs help your company site rank higher in search engines for important industry keyword phrases and blogs build a relationship with your customer by offering value.

When used effectively, a blog can help your company's site rank highly in Google for the most important keyword phrases in your industry. Forget about mind share, today Google share is a far greater asset for your business. For many product categories, no one knows who number one is in the category, so people often use Google to find out. Therefore owning real estate on the first page of search results is immensely important for marketing.

While blogs are not the only way to rank well in Google, they can provide a tremendous boost to your site through generation of lots of fresh content that att racts quality links. Sites with blogs oft enrank higher than sites without blogs because Google's algorithm considers frequency of updates, number of pages and number of links important factors in ranking. Hubspot conducted a survey of 1,531 businesses in which 795 of the businesses in the sample blogged and 736 didn't. The companies that blogged received 97 percent more inbound links, 434 percent more indexed pages and 55 percent more visitors (see http://bit.ly/5a5gab).

Blogs can also help potential customers to like and trust you because you are providing value through useful, interesting, or entertaining information. Your blog can have how-to articles, answers to common customer questions, lists of useful information (like "Top 10 Ways to Save Money"), discussions of interesting news and trends in the industry, and interviews of interesting people. An excellent company blog can make you the trusted source for valuable information in your industry, while creating positive feelings toward your brand.

COOLMARKETINGSTUFF.com

Batter Up: Get Busy Pitching Social Media

Jeff Cutler

The biggest challenge I've faced in pitching social media has been the impact argument.

Simply put, the impact argument is what individuals use when debating the worth of taking resources off a project that has demonstrable impact, and putting that money or those employees on social media assignments.

As an example, a cafe and catering business talked to me about using social media in their industry. They were purveyors of fabulous meals, had their catering operation spinning like a top, but they wanted an extra edge from social media.

My pitch went something like this:

1. How have you revised your marketing plan to include social media?
2. What resources are you willing to dedicate to these objectives?
3. Are you willing to wait nine months before seeing any impact, and longer before experiencing measurable ROI?

"Nine months?"

"Social media is supposed to be free."

"This isn't in our marketing budget."

I proceeded to inform them that:

- Social media *is* (in most cases) just one component of a complete marketing plan.
- Social media *does* require resources to be effective and it *does* take a lot of time.
- Social media *is not* a silver bullet that can create success where other traditional methods have failed.
- Social media *won't* save a bad product or a poorly run company.
- Social media *does* work when done correctly.

I wasn't giving a dog and pony show of who's following whom on Twitter and how to get a follower base to visit their restaurant. It wasn't a magic methods seminar on how SEO will drive everyone and their mother to their door. And I stopped short of promising results.

What I could promise — and this is what you can promise to your prospective clients when you're out pitching — is that you'll be able to measure impact. You'll be able to engage their customers who are already in the social media space. And you'll be able to get a percentage of those engagements to turn into sales and measurable ROI.

Beyond that, social media is just another tool in your marketing arsenal. When done right, it can work.

To pitch properly, you need to treat social media strategically. It's just one more way to communicate. And the more effectively you communicate how social media fits in to an overall marketing plan, the more clients you'll land.

Pitching Social Media

Valerie Simon

When I was in elementary school, once a week we would bring in a special book or toy from home. In first grade we called that time "Show and Tell." In second grade, it was referred to as "Sharing." At the time, I didn't think much about the difference between "Show and Tell" and "Sharing." Today, I understand that the distinction between the two is the key to effective PR 2.0.

By its very definition, a pitch is an attempt to sell, win approval, persuade or convince … in other words push a controlled message rather than engage in a conversation. The mindset of "pitching" stories has to change. Stop thinking about you, your client, your product, and how to position your story to the media. There is no effective way to *pitch* social media. It's time to graduate from "Show and Tell" to "Sharing."

Technorati's 2009 Annual State of the Blogosphere, asked 2,828 bloggers, "Why do you blog?" Seventy-one percent of those bloggers responded that they blog in order to speak their minds. In order to successfully engage these bloggers, and other social media influencers, it is critical to pay attention to what is currently on their minds and how you (or the product/service/client you represent) can respond to *their* needs. Share, educate, and be comfortable allowing influencers to draw their own conclusions and speak their mind.

Here are tips to help you move from the mindset of "Show and Tell" to "Sharing":

- **Look** — while you must still identify influentials, do not limit yourself to a few top targets with a large reach. Pay close attention to those bloggers in the "Magic Middle" who are conversing directly with your customers and other influentials

- **Listen** — social media strategists must take listening to a new level. Social media it is not a one way communication, and in order to succeed, you must understand that you don't always get to pick the topic of conversation. When customers share, they determine the subject matter. Customer service is an essential element in social media activity.

- **Contribute** — be acutely aware of the difference between educating and selling. Focus on how you can add value and support others. Make an effort to build the trust of not only influentials, but the community.

- **Inspire** — the goal is not simply to talk to your audience, but to get your audience talking. Focus on building relationships and developing true enthusiasts.

EXAMINER.com/x-5725-Public-Relations-Examiner

Pitching Social Media

Jeff Garrison

When my clients say, "I don't *get* social media," they really mean that they don't *appreciate* social media — at least not the way most enthusiasts pitch it — as a strategy. Social media is not a strategy; it's a tactic.

Look at it this way: once upon a time, the objective of businesses was to increase sales. Part of their marketing strategy was to make themselves easily-findable by people looking for their product, service, or company name. A tactic they might use was buying an ad in the yellow pages. ("I am somebody!" as Steve Martin said in The Jerk, after seeing his name in the phone book for the first time.) To make the best use of this tactic, many businesses would buy a bigger space or red lettering, or even place a logo or picture.

Today, increasing sales is still the business objective. Being easily findable is still part of the strategy. But the tactics have changed.

So if Google and corporate websites have replaced the phone book, what is social media? Social media is like the big ad, the red lettering, the logos and pictures that just jump off the page and grab the prospect.

Your prospects can get to know your company through your website. But they will know you better and come to like and trust you through your blog, your Twitter posts, your Facebook page, and your YouTube videos. You "Digg?"

If that is not reason enough to consider social media as a tactic that will enhance your business strategy, think about this. With the yellow pages, you could only be first in your category if your company name was "AA" something. Additionally, once they were on the page, you could not push your competition off the page. With social media, you can become the most "relevant" in your category and therefore number one on the list. You can also be number two, three, four, and so on in a Google search. You can push your competition right off the page!

Pitch that!

JCGARRISON.com

Pitching Social to Artists: Connecting Artists and Customers — Without a Gallery

Lori A. Magno

Artists and artisans have long needed gallery and shop owners to provide a steady stream of customers and income. Benefactors are nice, but oh-so-rare.

Thanks to the social media age, artists stand a greater chance at success than they did just ten years ago. Success can mean a life-sustaining volume of sales with a little notoriety thrown in (Hi Mom!), or it can mean growing your street art into an impressive and totally vertically-controlled empire.

Contemporary artist Shepard Fairey grew from street artist to guerilla marketer and successful sticker seller to having a top-selling political poster and show at the Institute of Contemporary Art in Boston. It wasn't overnight success, but he controlled his product and his destiny. He connected with his audience and he understood social.

It hasn't been difficult to "pitch" social to artists. The number of sites that will host an artist's shop has exploded. You've probably heard of Etsy, ArtFire or 1000 Markets, but international artisan sites like Folksy, MISI and Dawanda have sprung up in the last two years, and they are seeing exponential growth and fanatical shoppers.

Artists are embracing social tools and sites like ArtFire, which have embraced a holistic approach to social. Each seller's site features a blog page and gallery tools, but from each item-page you can link to an artist's Blogger page, Flickr, Facebook, Twitter, and even the artist's Etsy shop. (How's *that* for embracing social!)

Etsy, ArtFire, Zibbet, and Big Cartel offer streams of ideas for artists to promote their work using social media. Each site has a community forum where artists exchange ideas and technical tips or just vent. Their leaders are on Twitter and Facebook, speaking directly to the community, and artists love the connection with customers and other artists.

The exciting thing for artists is that these sites are in serious competition with each other. ArtFire is connected with Amazon, making it possible to save items to your Amazon Wish List. Etsy and ArtFire have nifty Facebook apps, and everyone is working on mobile.

These sites are happy to help artists sell their seashell ashtrays, hand-wrought jewelry, or polymer clay gewgaws, all at a 3.5 percent commission. Which is significantly better than a 60-40 split any day.

LORIMAGNO.com

Pitching Social Media

Dr. Letitia Wright

This is how I describe social media: It's a few of your friends and family who truly love and care about you, mixed in with thousands of people shouting to sell you something. Social media was developed differently from the rest of media — TV, radio, magazines and newspapers. The rules are different, the expectations are different.

The idea of pitching your irresistible viral video, having all of social media embrace it and getting millions of plays, thus creating millions of dollars in revenue, is just another internet urban legend. There are videos that go viral: The Validation Video, The Evolution of Dance, Single Babies and Otters holding hands have had millions of views, but none of these have any commercial significance. They don't sell anything and don't really advocate for anything. You cannot make a viral video. You make a video that you hope people will embrace and viewers decide it's viral. Viewers share it with their friends. If someone is about to sell you a viral video that will introduce your products to the social media sphere, get your money back. You don't get to choose if it's viral. Only the audience does.

Pitching social media is never going to have a formula. It is in constant flux because humans are constantly changing it. The only thing that works across the board is relationship. Create real relationships. There are friends and friendlies. Friendlies are those who sign up, they follow and may do the basic interaction, in order to get you to reciprocate. Friendlies won't buy from you, they won't send money to your favorite charity, and they won't support you in any tangible way. They are friendlies, connected to you on social media for the benefit of being connected.

Then there are friends. Friends will rally behind what you are doing, and contribute to a cause because they know and trust you. So when you are pitching social media, you have to have strong enough relationships to make it work. Loose ties to people who will not notice if you don't pop up in their stream are not good for expanding your business.

So how do you pitch social media? You don't. You don't pitch social media; you pitch your personal contacts. You do pitch your friends and supporters. This list is a lot smaller than your lists in social media, and it will also be far more effective.

WRIGHTPLACETV.com

Social Media Is the New CRM

Riku Vassinen

I did my master´s thesis about CRM systems, and ended up working with social media. So I have been jumping from one hype to another. Social media and CRM share lots of similar traits, both good and bad.

1. Social Media and CRM Are Both Buzzwords

Your boss is talking about social media, your clients are talking about social media and you are talking about social media. No one really knows what it means. And let me guess, the CRM-project you started four years ago is still not ready?

2. They Are Both Based on Simple Things

CRM is about knowing your customers better. Social media is about conversations between people. Social media is about going where your potential audience is — talking with them in their own language, not using corporate jargon.

3. They Are About People, Not Technology

The biggest social media is still email, not Facebook or Twitter. The biggest CRM system is Excel, not SAP or Siebel. If you use them properly, they are all you need to get by. If you just want to test out new technologies, stay away from social media. Buy SAP instead.

4. Most Projects Totally Fail

Seventy to ninety percent of CRM projects totally fail, and probably the same percentage of new social media initiatives fail. Maybe even more. Many companies fail to understand that CRM and social media are about change management. You have to sell the idea of participating in these programs. Too often we forget that because we are excited about everything new and technology-related. You were excited about the upcoming CRM-project, weren´t you?

5. When Done Right, Companies Can Gain Competitive Advantage with Them

With social media you can engage better with your potential and existing customers. Eventually, you can even convert them into your fans. There are no quick wins, but when you incorporate social media into your corporate DNA, you can gain competitive advantage, which is really hard for by competitors to replicate. Nowadays, the only thing helping you stand out from the competition is your fans. Ask Apple.

A reality check: the investment in social media initiatives is only a fraction of the price of the new CRM system. And it is done much more rapidly.

Do believe the hype.

PIMPMYCONTENT.BLOGSPOT.com

Picking the Social Media Vehicle That Is Right for Your Business

Deborah Chaddock Brown

So many social media choices, so little time. It's overwhelming. I have an hour. Do I write a blog post, read some tweets, check status updates on LinkedIn, visit my Facebook page or read my RSS feeds?

It can be overwhelming and that's why social media has gotten a reputation as the procrastinator's favorite pastime. However, the value of building relationships and connecting with peers via the internet is worth figuring out how to add it to your schedule. Kind of like exercise but more fun.

- What do I want to accomplish with Social Media?
- What results do I expect?

Connect with your customers — social media is a great place to start.

1. Set up Google Alerts for your name and the name of your company. Respond quickly to positive and negative comments.
2. Create a Facebook page for your business which links to all of your web touch points (blog, articles, newsletters, LinkedIn and Twitter accounts).
3. Use the same name consistently for all your social media accounts so customers can easily find you.
4. Use Twitter to keep customers updated on changes to your business and most importantly, leave tweets if there is a problem customers need to be aware of.
5. Use all of your social media platforms to invite comments, suggestions, opinions and ideas. The best business is one built on the needs of the customer — social media allows you to have conversations with your prospects and customers.
6. Provide value with blog postings that share tips, trends and techniques for being more successful, saving money, going Green, or being more efficient.

Establish your expert status — blogging, commenting on other blogs, writing articles, answering questions on LinkedIn, leaving comments on forums, writing book reviews on Amazon, and sharing links to valuable resources through Facebook, LinkedIn and Twitter can all keep your name in front of prospects. Each action results in an indexed page that is connected to your name.

Make money — there are plenty of affiliate programs, sponsored ads and get-rich programs to pick from. Just Google them.

Before you get started, make sure you understand what you want from social media and then select the vehicle that will allow you to be successful and provide value to your customers.

ALLWRITEINK.com
MAKEORBREAKMOMENTS.com/blog

LaVergne, TN USA
11 June 2010
185903LV00001B/25/P

9 780982 473948